**EASY PIANO**

# THE DISNEY COLLECTION

*Best-loved Songs From Disney Movies,*

*Television Shows and Theme Parks*

P9-CPX-244

© The Walt Disney Company

ISBN 978-0-7935-0830-3

HAL•LEONARD™ CORPORATION

7777 W. BLUEMOUND RD. P.O. BOX 13819 MILWAUKEE, WI 53213

# THE DISNEY COLLECTION

## Alphabetical Listing

# THE DISNEY COLLECTION

This listing matches the sequence of the songs on the three recorded albums of
THE DISNEY COLLECTION, released by Walt Disney Records and available in your local record stores.

## VOLUME 1

## VOLUME 2

## VOLUME 3

# BABY MINE
## (From Walt Disney's "DUMBO")

Words by NED WASHINGTON
Music by FRANK CHURCHILL

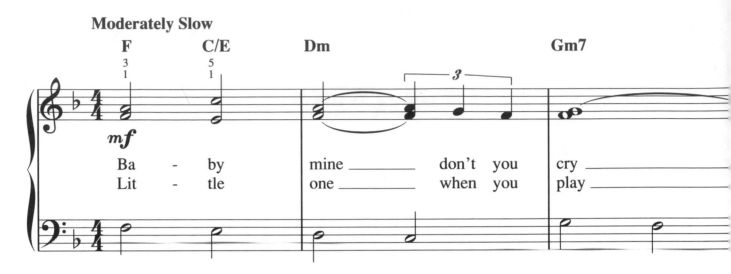

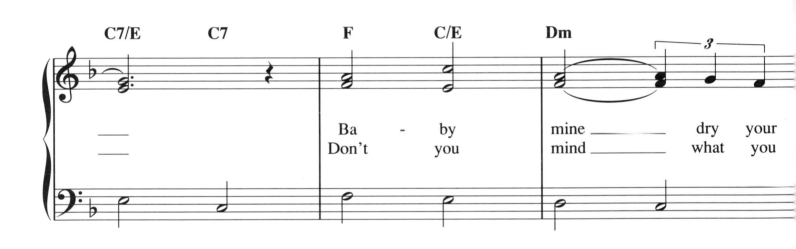

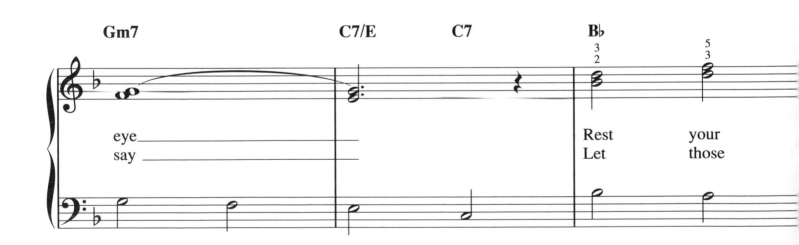

Gm7

head        close    to    my
eyes        spar - kle    and

Gm

heart,      nev - er    to
shine       nev - er    a

Gdim

part,       Ba - by    of
tear,       Ba - by    of

F

mine. _____
mine. _____

1.

2.

**Slightly Faster**
Dm

If        they

knew    sweet lit - tle    you _____

Em7sus

A7

_____

Dm

They'd        end    up    lov - ing    you

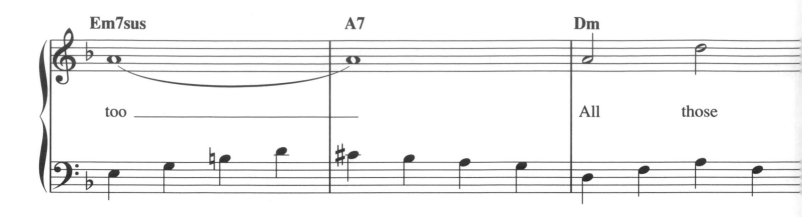

too _____ All those

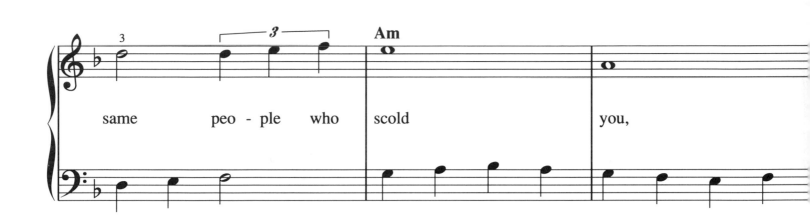

same peo - ple who scold you,

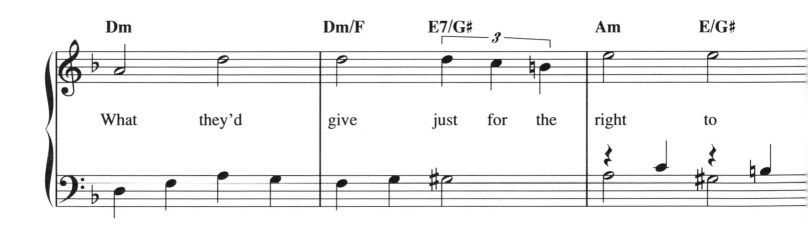

What they'd give just for the right to hold

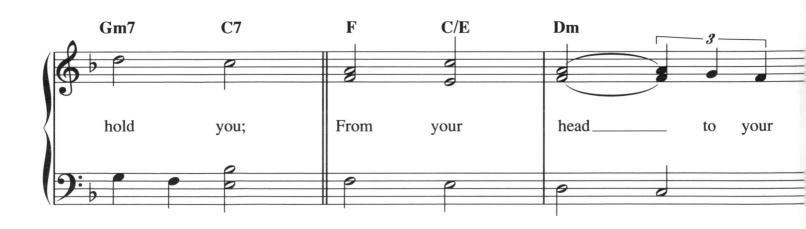

hold you; From your head_____ to your

# THE BALLAD OF DAVY CROCKETT

## (From "DAVY CROCKETT, KING OF THE WILD FRONTIER")

Words by TOM BLACKBURN
Music by GEORGE BRUNS

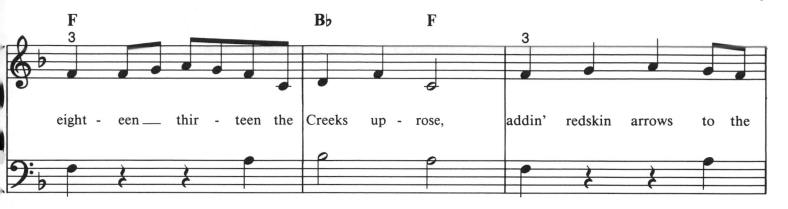

eight - een — thir - teen the Creeks up - rose, addin' redskin arrows to the

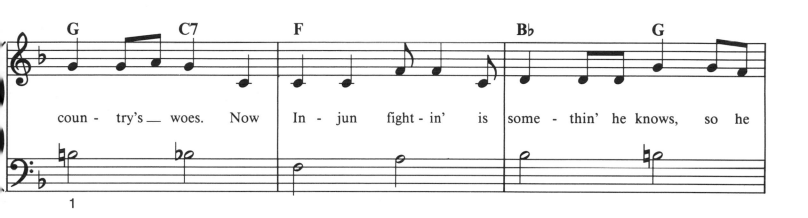

coun - try's — woes. Now In - jun fight - in' is some - thin' he knows, so he

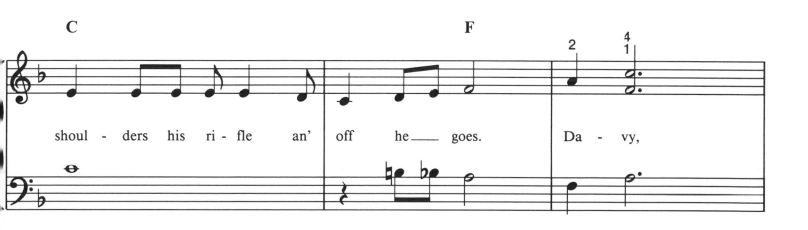

shoul - ders his ri - fle an' off he — goes. Da - vy,

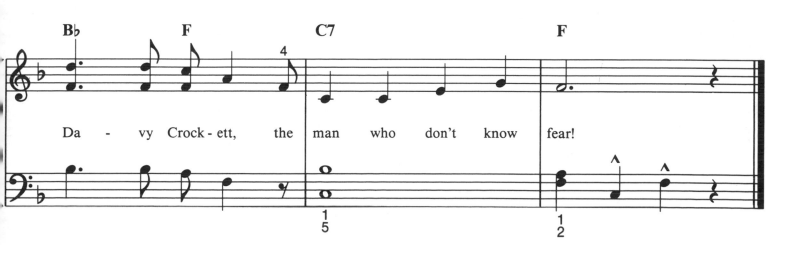

Da - vy Crock - ett, the man who don't know fear!

# THE BARE NECESSITIES
## (From Walt Disney's "THE JUNGLE BOOK")

Words and Music by
TERRY GILKYSON

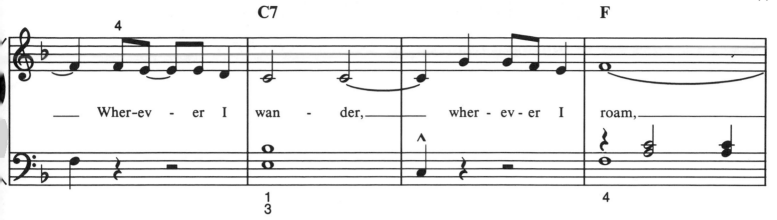

Wher-ev - er I wan - der,___ wher - ev - er I roam,___

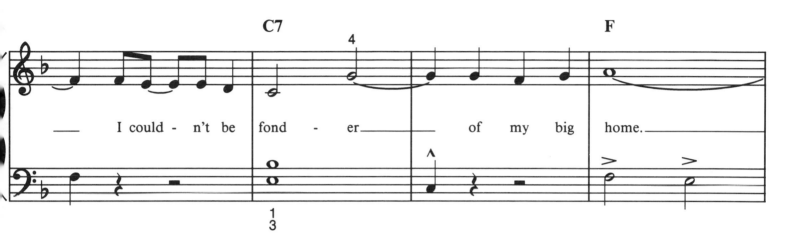

___ I could - n't be fond - er___ of my big home.___

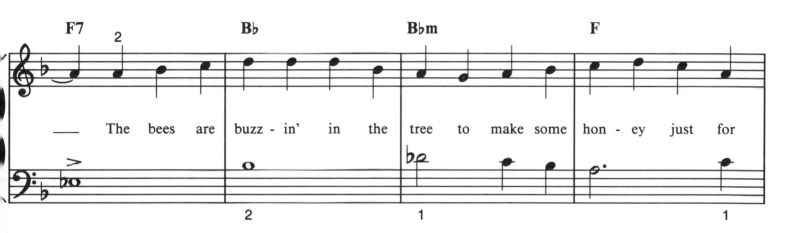

___ The bees are buzz - in' in the tree to make some hon - ey just for

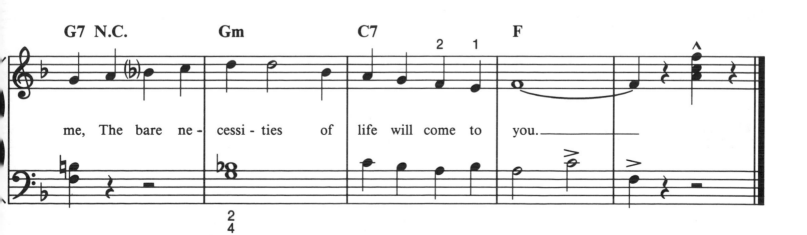

me, The bare ne - cessi - ties of life will come to you.___

# BELLA NOTTE

## (From Walt Disney's "LADY AND THE TRAMP")

Words and Music by PEGGY LE
and SONNY BURK

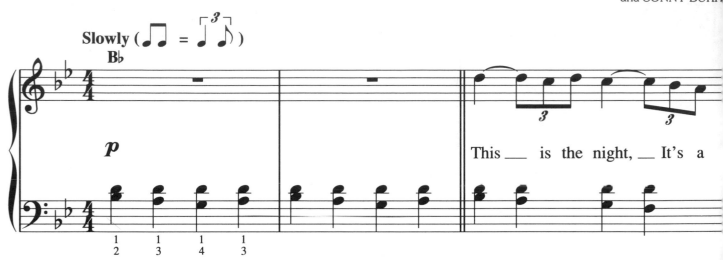

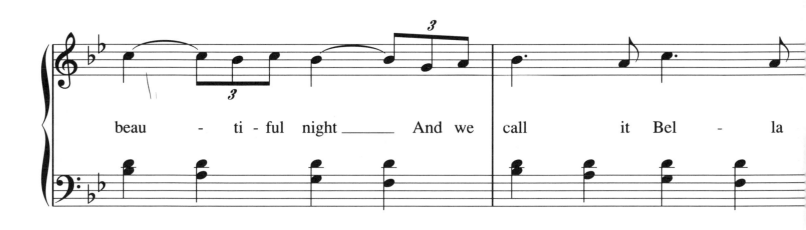

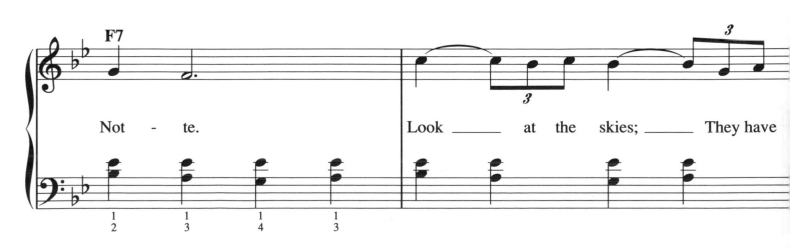

stars _____ in their eyes _____ On this love - ly Bel - la

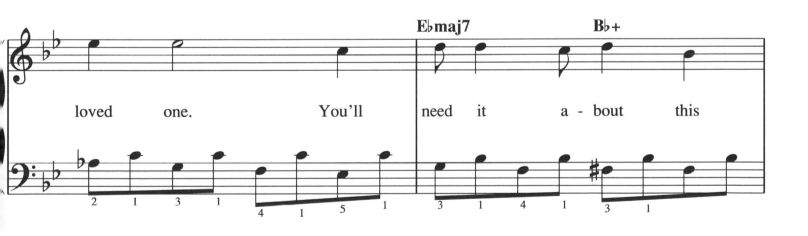

Not - te. So take this love _____ of your

loved one. You'll need it a - bout this

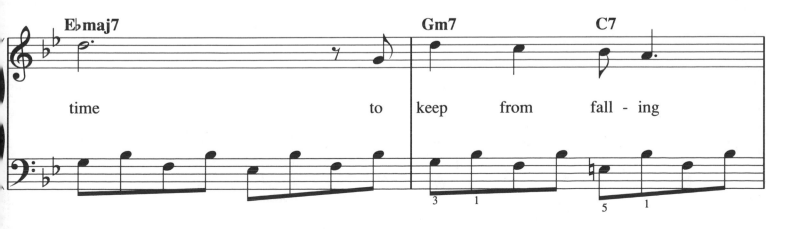

time to keep from fall - ing

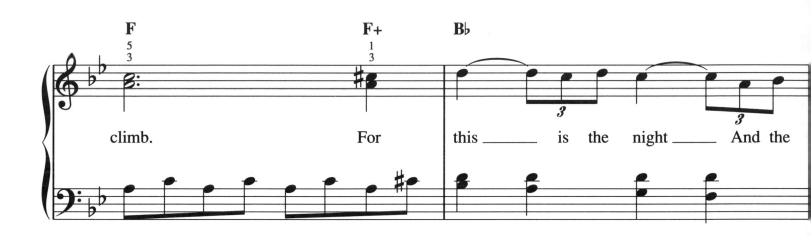

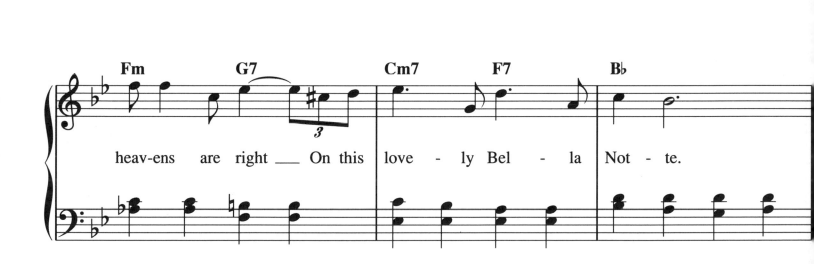

# Bibbidi-Bobbidi-Boo
## (From Walt Disney's "CINDERELLA")

Words by JERRY LIVINGSTON
Music by MACK DAVID and AL HOFFMAN

**Light Schottische**

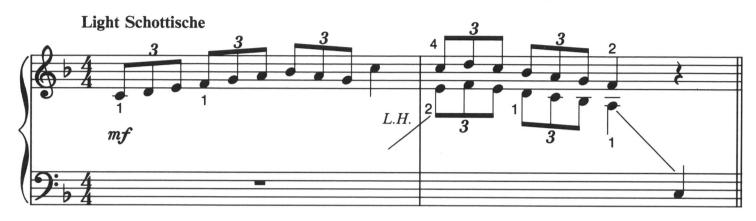

Sa - la - ga - doo - la men - chic - ka boo - la, Bib - bi - di - Bob - bi - di - Boo.

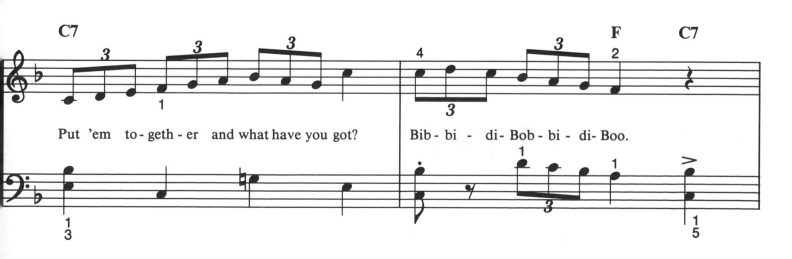

Put 'em to - geth - er and what have you got? Bib - bi - di - Bob - bi - di - Boo.

16

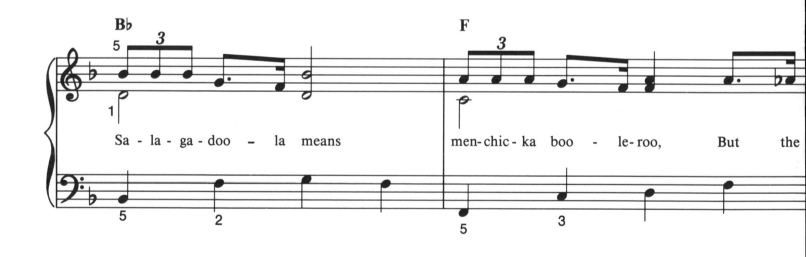

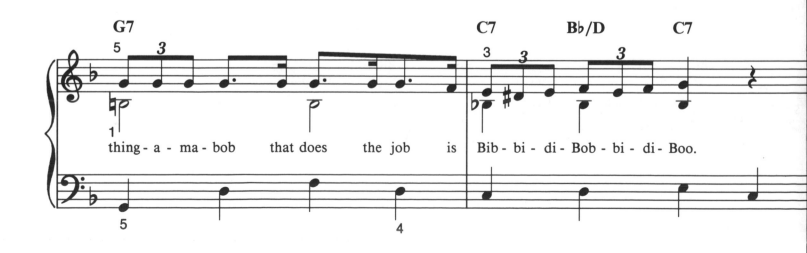

# BEST OF FRIENDS

(From Walt Disney's "THE FOX AND THE HOUND")

Words by STAN FIDE
Music by RICHARD JOHNSTO

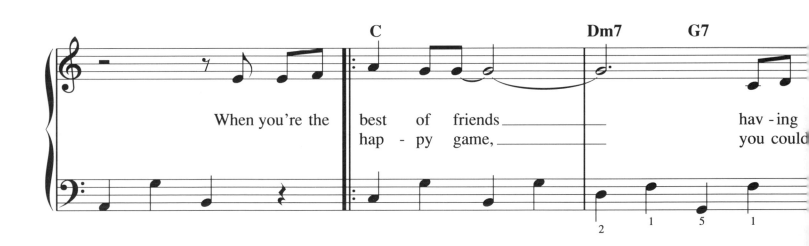

When you're the | best of friends _____ | hav-ing
hap - py game, _____ | you could

so much fun to-geth - er | you're not e - ven a - ware_ you're such a
clown a - round for ev - er. | Nei - ther one of you sees_ your nat-ur'l

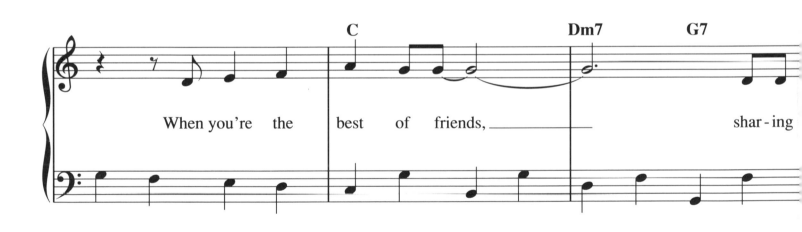

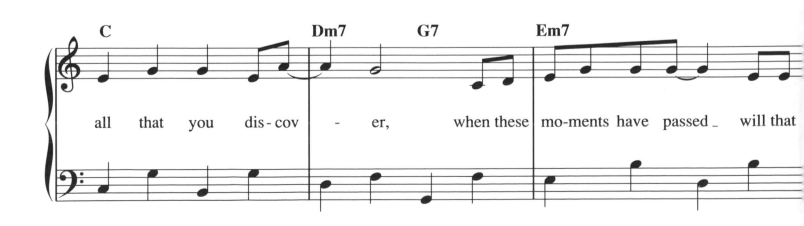

friend - ship last? __ Who can say __ if there's a way? __

How I hope, __ I hope it nev - er ends, __

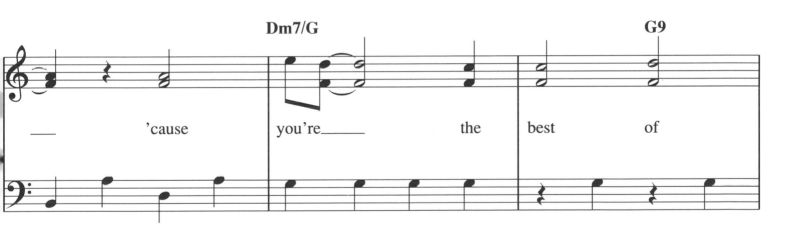

__ 'cause you're __ the best of

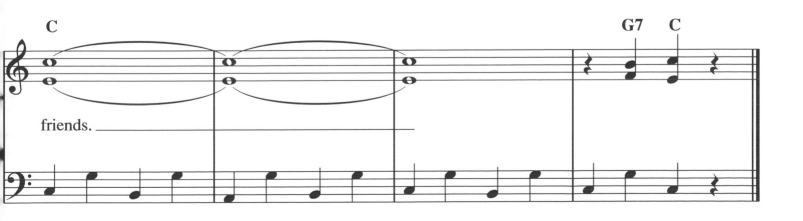

friends. __

# CANDLE ON THE WATER

## (From Walt Disney Productions "PETE'S DRAGON")

Words and Music by AL KASH
and JOEL HIRSCHHOF

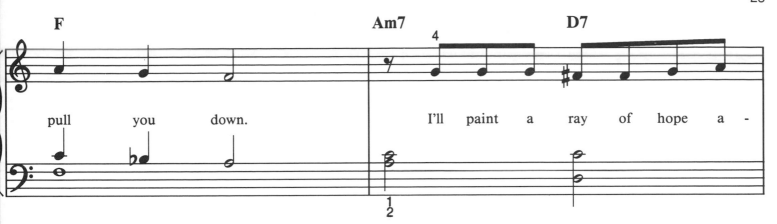

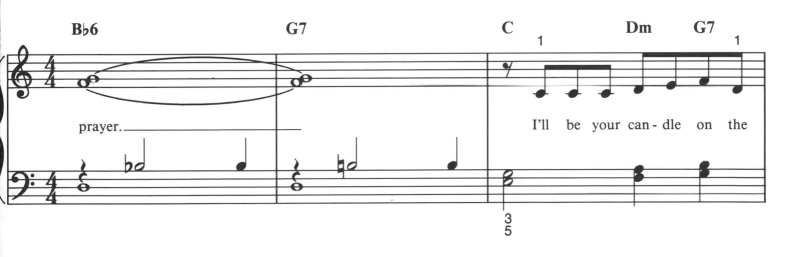

on,     you'll make it;     Here's my hand so take it,     look for me     reach-ing out to

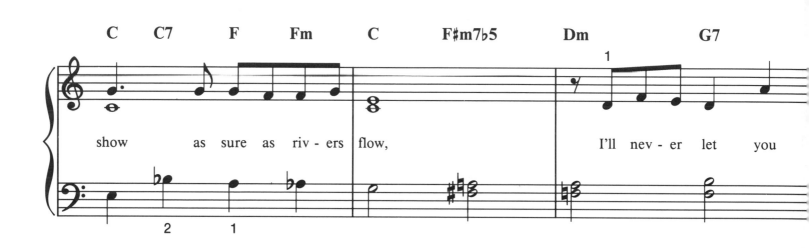

show          as sure as riv-ers |flow,          I'll nev-er let     you

go,          I'll nev-er let     you     go,          I'll nev-er let     you

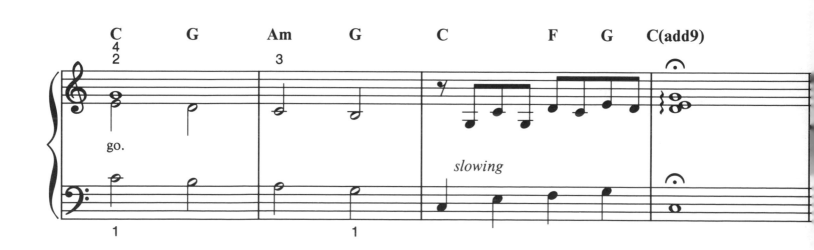

go.                                        slowing

# CASEY JUNIOR
## (From Walt Disney's "DUMBO")

Words by NED WASHINGTON
Music by FRANK CHURCHILL

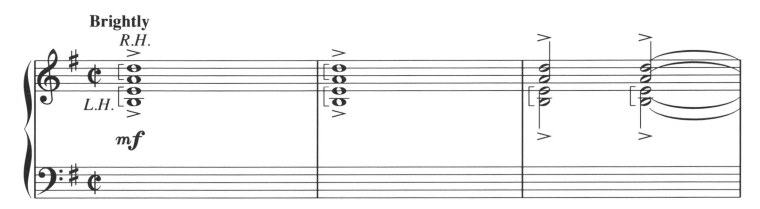

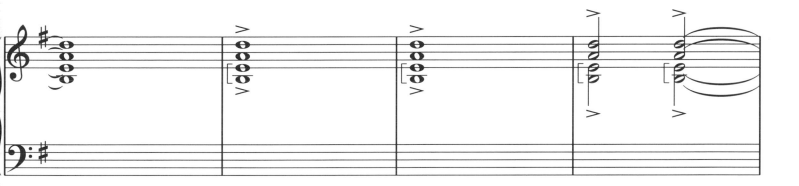

It's
Hear

Cas - ey Jun - ior com - in'
him puff - in'

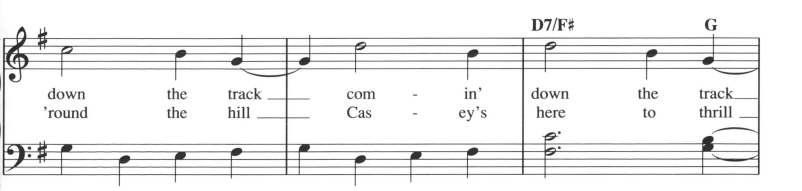

down the track com - in' down the track
'round the hill Cas - ey's here to thrill

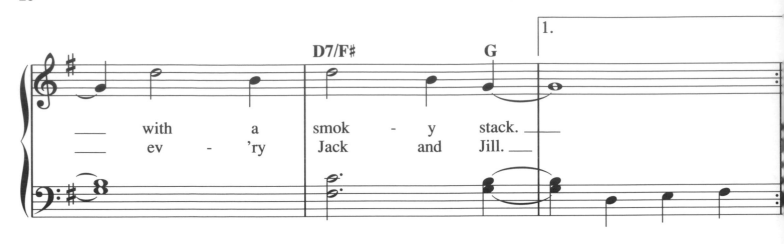

with a smok - y stack. ___
ev - 'ry Jack and Jill. ___

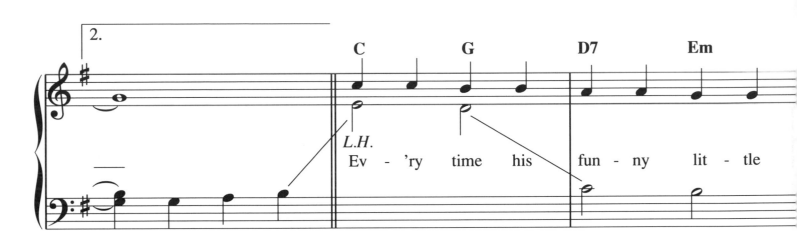

*L.H.*
Ev - 'ry time his fun - ny lit - tle

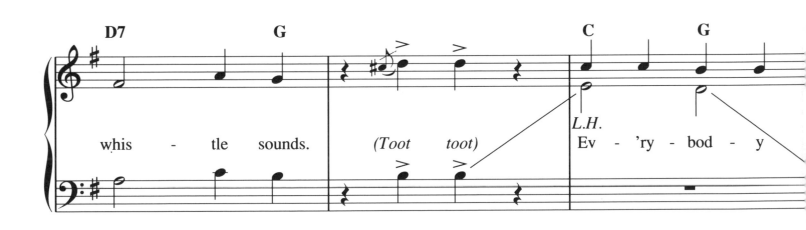

whis - tle sounds. *(Toot toot)*
*L.H.*
Ev - 'ry - bod - y

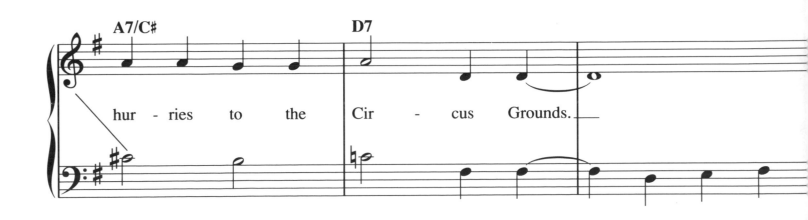

hur - ries to the Cir - cus Grounds. ___

27

Words - 1st 2 pg.

# CRUELLA DE VIL
## (From Walt Disney's "ONE HUNDRED AND ONE DALMATIONS")

Words and Music b
MEL LEVE

Slow blues

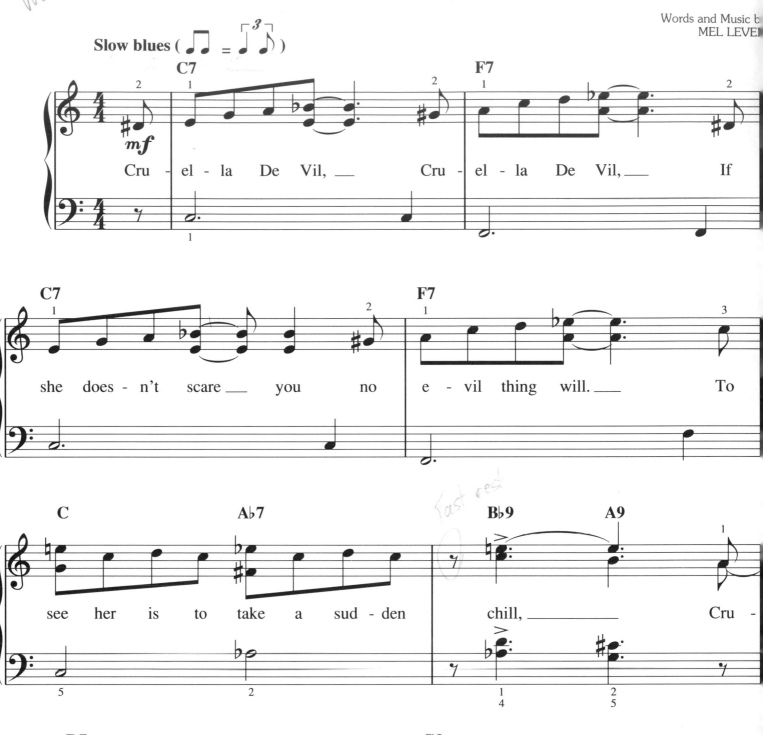

Cru - el - la De Vil, ____ Cru - el - la De Vil, ____ If

she does - n't scare ____ you no e - vil thing will. ____ To

see her is to take a sud - den chill, ____ Cru -

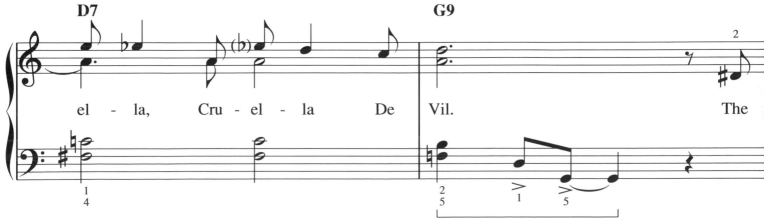

el - la, Cru - el - la De Vil. The

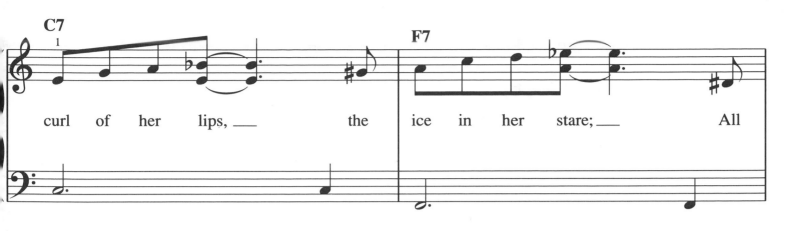

curl of her lips, ___ the ice in her stare; ___ All

in - no - cent chil - dren had bet - ter be - ware. ___ She's

like a spi - der wait - ing for a kill. ___ Look

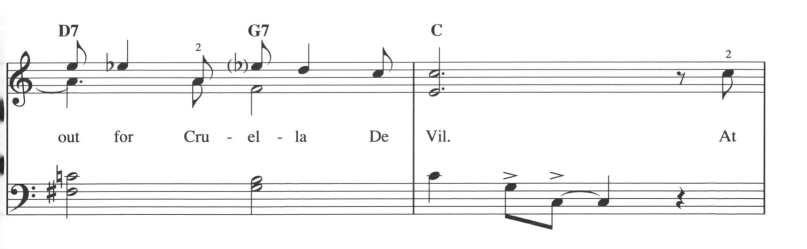

out for Cru - el - la De Vil. At

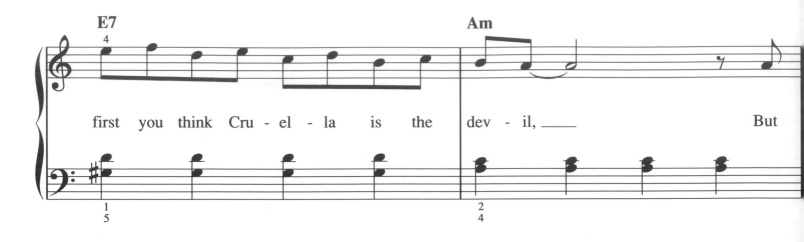

first you think Cru - el - la is the dev - il, ____ But

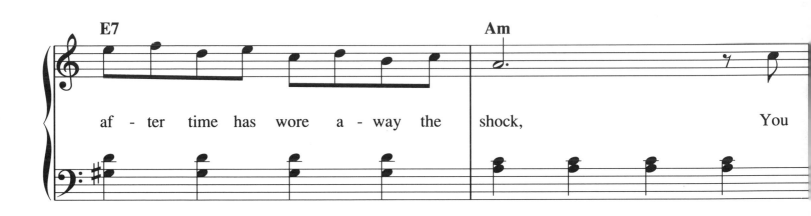

af - ter time has wore a - way the shock, You

come to re - al - ize you've seen her kind of eyes

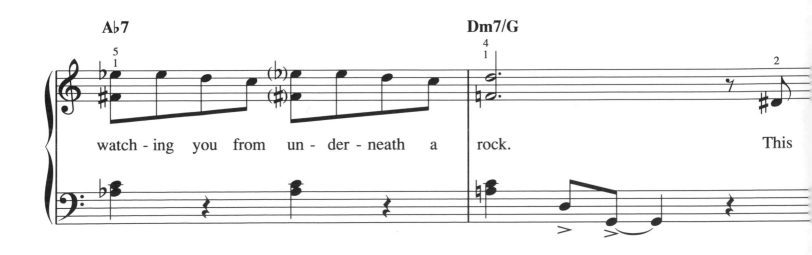

watch - ing you from un - der - neath a rock. This

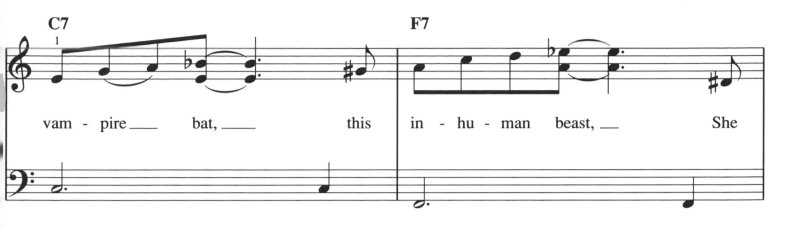

vam - pire ___ bat, ___ this in - hu - man beast, ___ She

ought to be locked ___ up and nev - er re - leased. ___ The

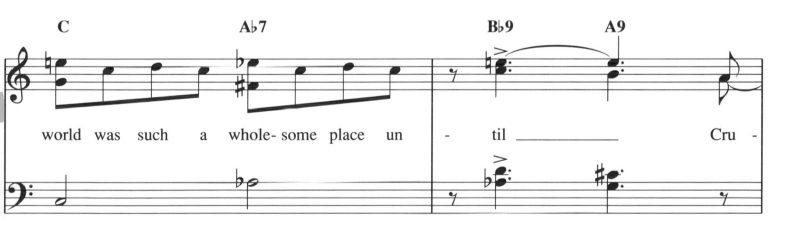

world was such a whole- some place un - til _____ Cru -

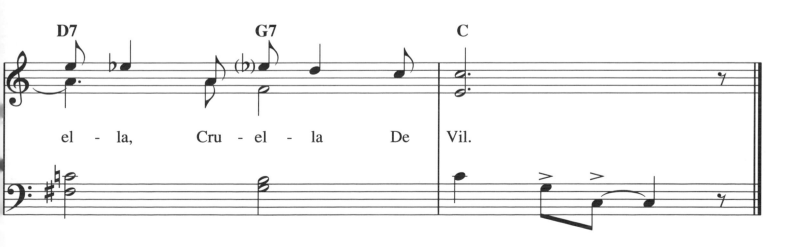

el - la, Cru - el - la De Vil.

# CHIM CHIM CHER-EE
## (From Walt Disney's "MARY POPPINS")

Words and Music by RICHARD M. SHERMAN
and ROBERT B. SHERMAN

Lightly, with gusto

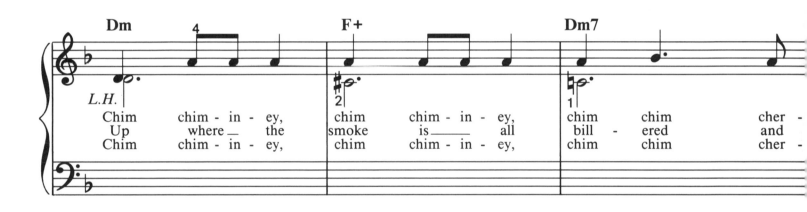

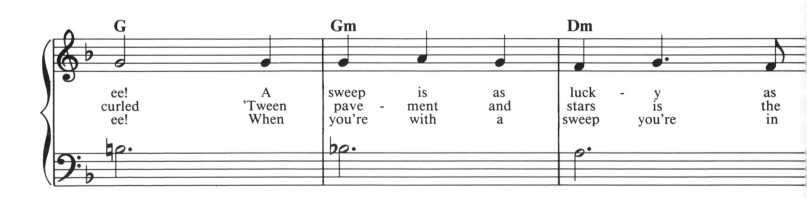

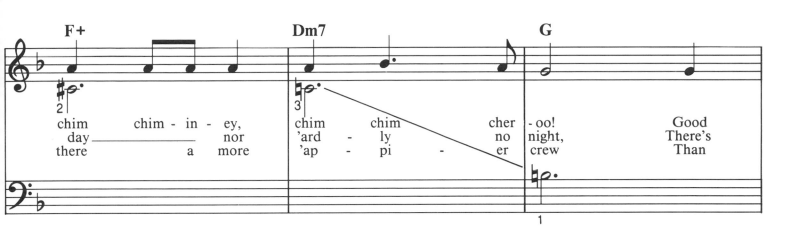

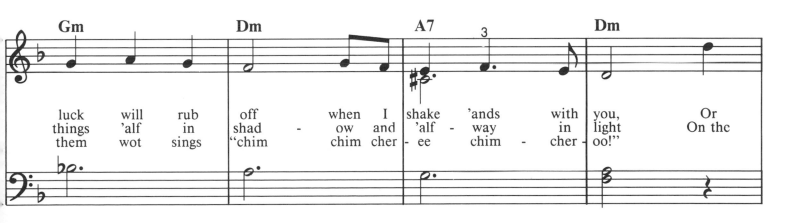

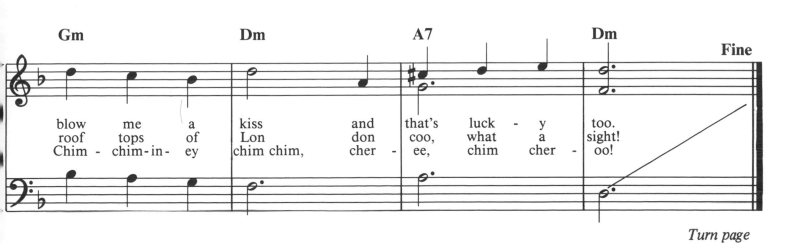

*Turn page*

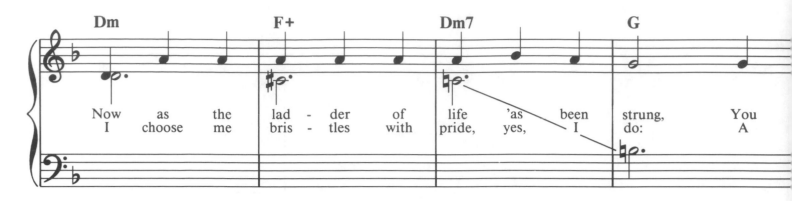

Now as the lad - der of life 'as been strung, You
I choose me bris - tles with pride, yes, I do: A

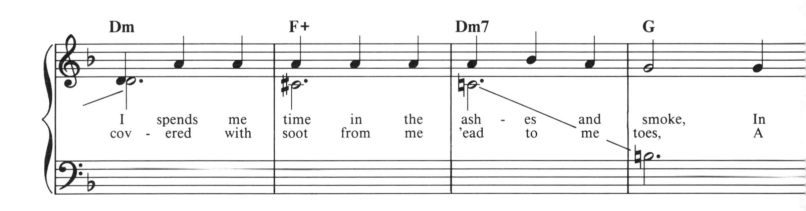

may think a sweep's on the bot - tom - most rung. Though
broom for the shaft and a brush for the flue. Though I'm

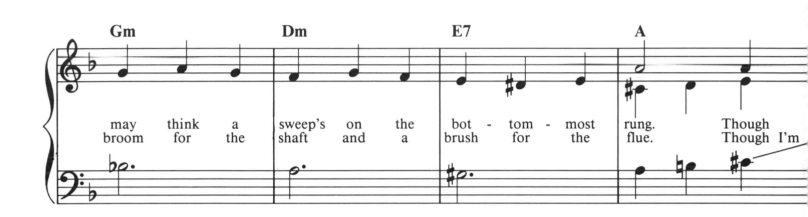

I spends me time in the ash - es and smoke, In
cov - ered with soot from me 'ead to me toes, A

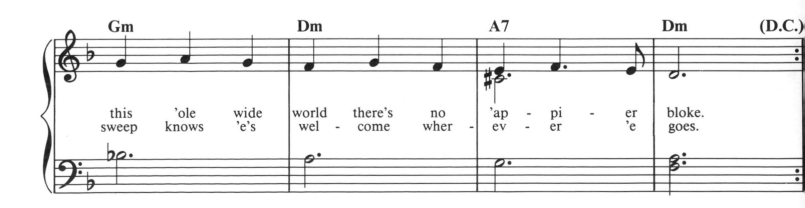

this 'ole wide world there's no 'ap - pi - er bloke.
sweep knows 'e's wel - come wher - ev - er 'e goes.

# EV'RYBODY WANTS TO BE A CAT

(From Walt Disney's "THE ARISTOCATS")

Words by FLOYD HUDDLESTON
Music by AL RINKER

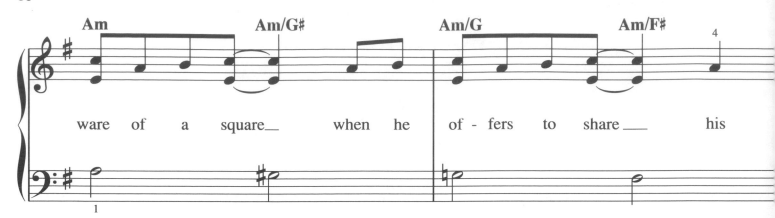

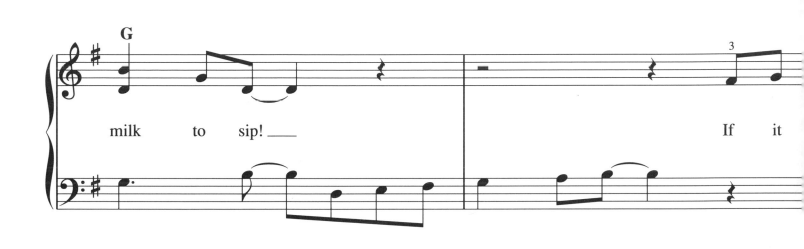

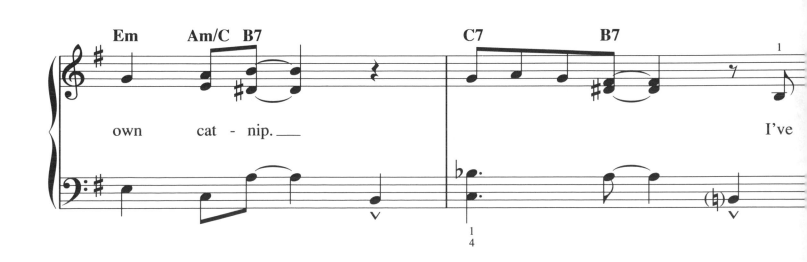

37

38

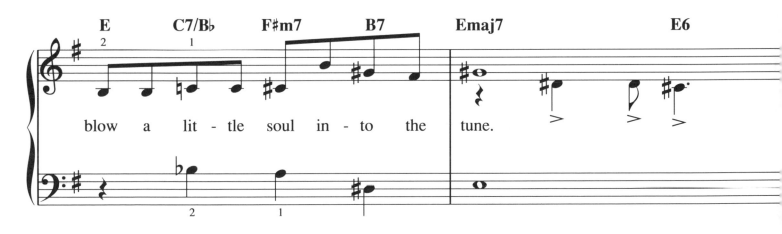

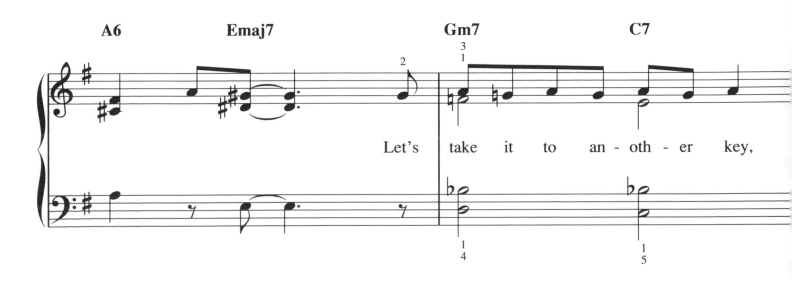

# A DREAM IS A WISH
# YOUR HEART MAKES

(From Walt Disney's "CINDERELLA")

Words and Music by MACK DAVID
AL HOFFMAN, and JERRY LIVINGSTON

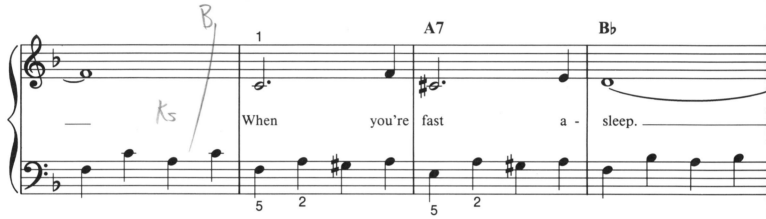

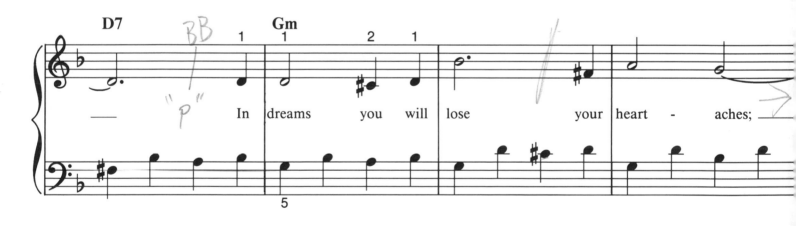

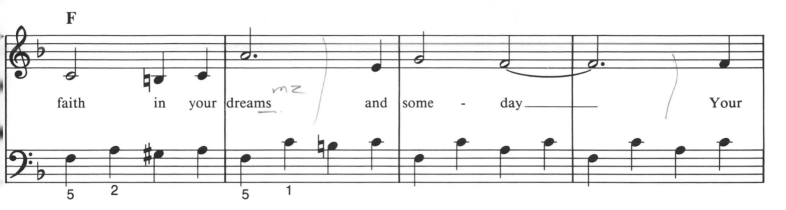

faith in your dreams and some - day Your

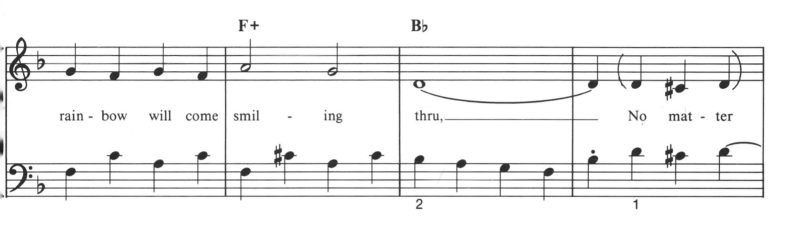

rain - bow will come smil - ing thru, No mat - ter

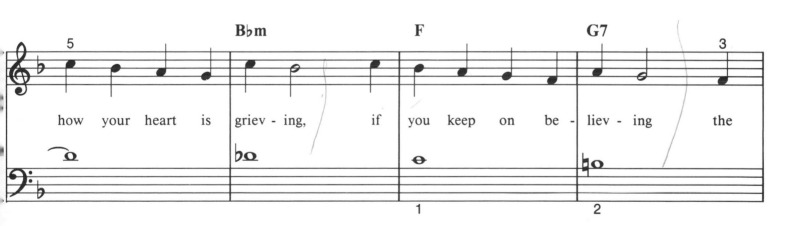

how your heart is griev - ing, if you keep on be - liev - ing the

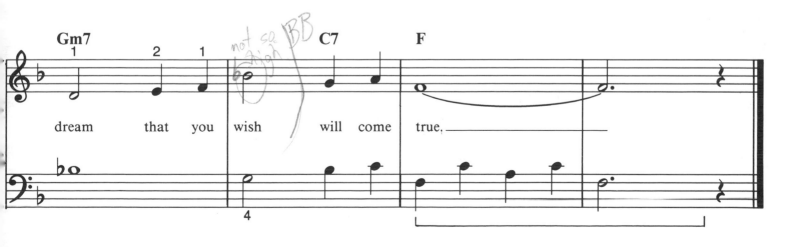

dream that you wish will come true,

# FEED THE BIRDS
## (From Walt Disney's "MARY POPPINS")

Words and Music by RICHARD M. SHERMAN
and ROBERT B. SHERMAN

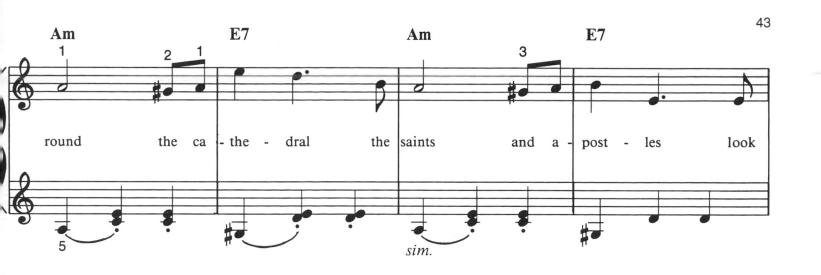

round the ca - the - dral the saints and a - post - les look

down as she sells her wares. _____ Al -

though you can't see it, you know they are smil - ing each

time some - one shows that he cares. _____

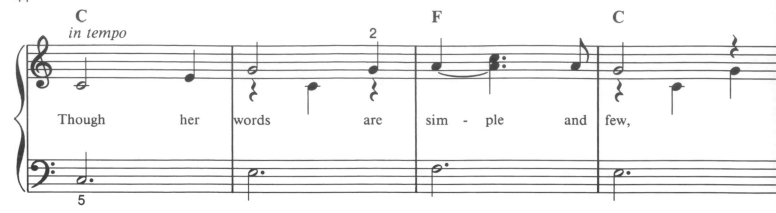

Though her words are sim - ple and few,

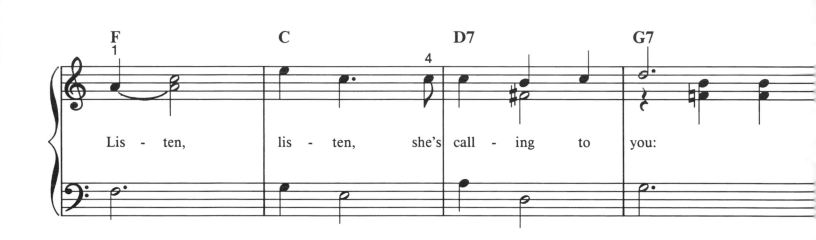

Lis - ten, lis - ten, she's call - ing to you:

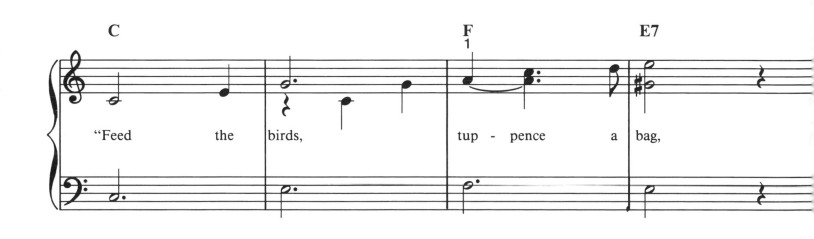

"Feed the birds, tup - pence a bag,

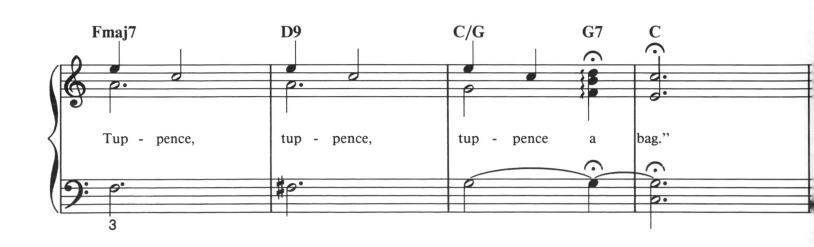

Tup - pence, tup - pence, tup - pence a bag."

# FOLLOWING THE LEADER

(From Walt Disney's "PETER PAN")

Words by TED SEARS and WINSTON HIBLER
Music by OLIVER WALLACE

**Gaily (in 2; ♩. = 1 beat)**

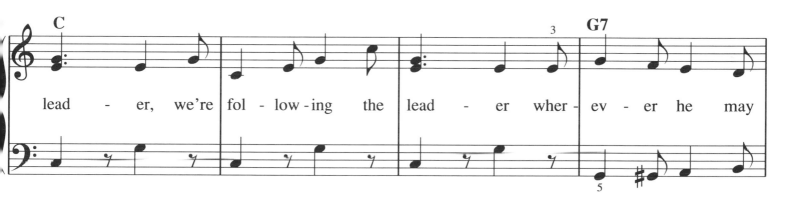

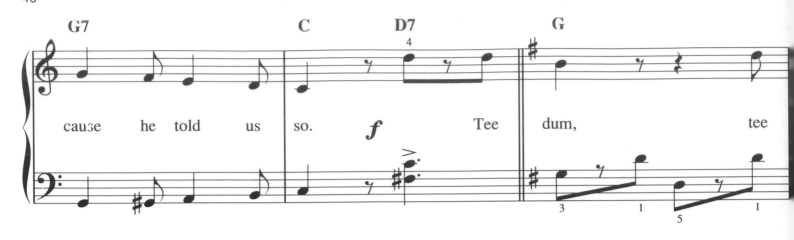

G7　　　　　　　　　　C　　　D7　　　　　G

cause　he　told　us　so.　　_f_　　　Tee　dum,　　　　tee

　　　　　　　　　　　　　　　　　　　　D7

dee,　　　　　a　tee-dle　ee　dō　tee　day.　　{ We're
　　　　　　　　　　　　　　　　　　　　　　　　We

out　　　　　for　fun　　　　and　this　is　the　game　we
march　　　　a - long　　　and　these　are　the　words　we

G　　　　　　　　　　　　　　　　　　　　　　3

play:　　　　Come　on,　　　　join　in　　　　and
say:　　　　Tee　dum,　　　tee　dee,　　　a

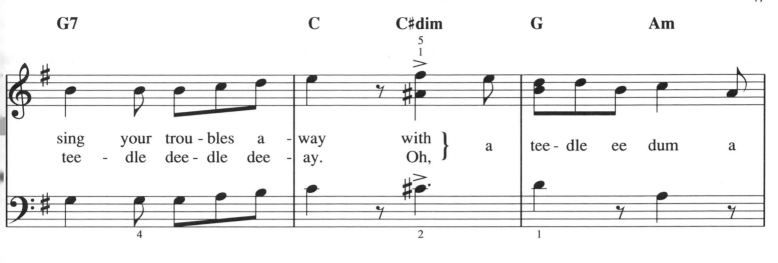

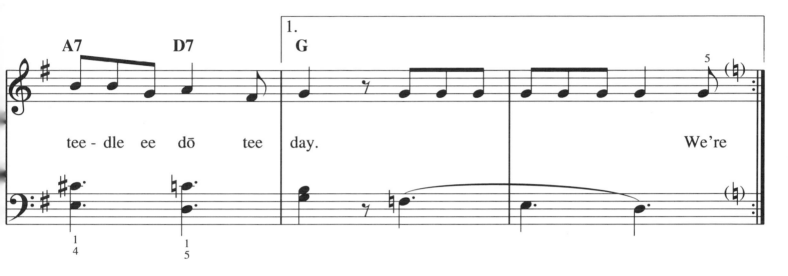

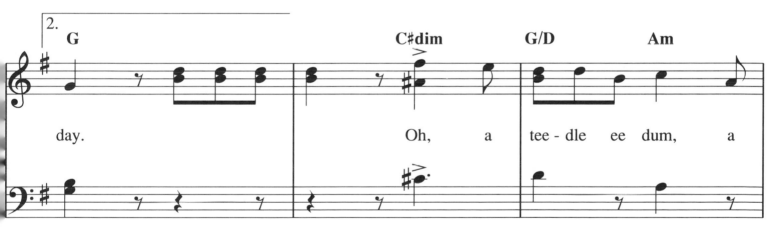

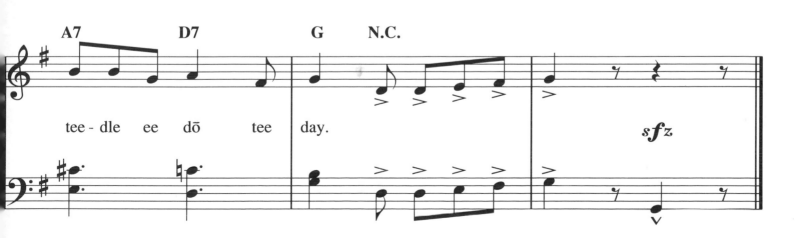

# GIVE A LITTLE WHISTLE

## (From Walt Disney's "PINOCCHIO")

Words by NED WASHINGTON
Music by LEIGH HARLINE

# HE'S A TRAMP

## (From Walt Disney's "LADY AND THE TRAMP")

Words and Music by PEGGY L
and SONNY BUR

51

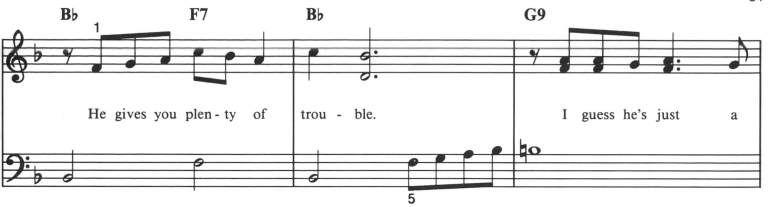

He gives you plen - ty of trou - ble. I guess he's just a

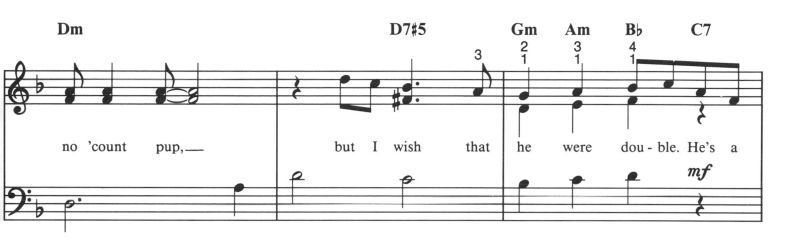

no 'count pup,— but I wish that he were dou - ble. He's a

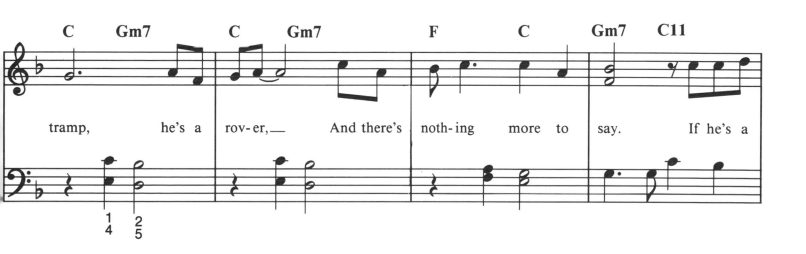

tramp, he's a rov-er,— And there's noth-ing more to say. If he's a

tramp, he's a good one,— And I wish that I could trav-el his way.

# HI-DIDDLE-DEE-DEE

## (An Actor's Life For Me)

## (From Walt Disney's "PINOCCHIO")

Words by NED WASHINGTON
Music by LEIGH HARLINE

53

# HEIGH-HO
## (The Dwarfs' Marching Song)
### (From Walt Disney's "SNOW WHITE AND THE SEVEN DWARFS")

Words by LARRY MOREY
Music by FRANK CHURCHILL

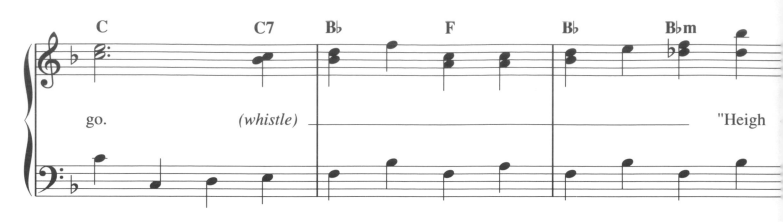

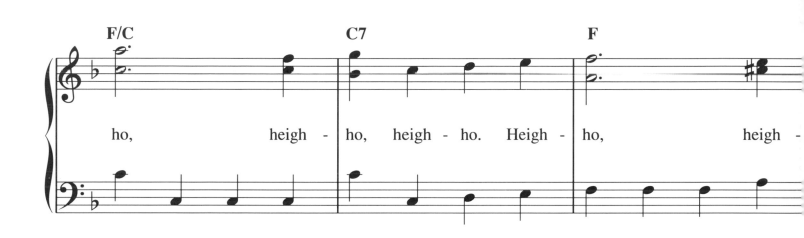

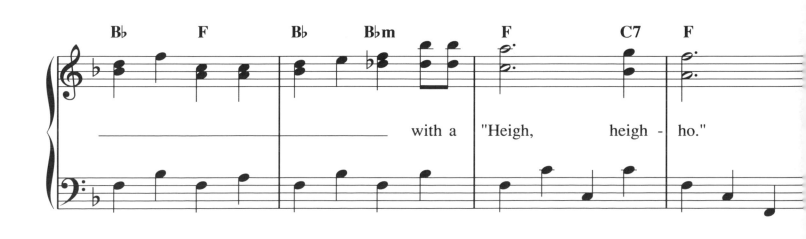

# I WAN'NA BE LIKE YOU

## (From Walt Disney's "THE JUNGLE BOOK")

Words and Music by RICHARD M. SHERMAN
and ROBERT B. SHERMAN

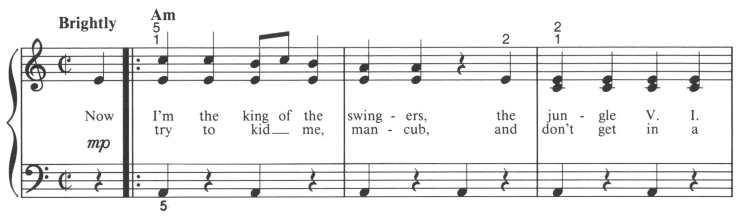

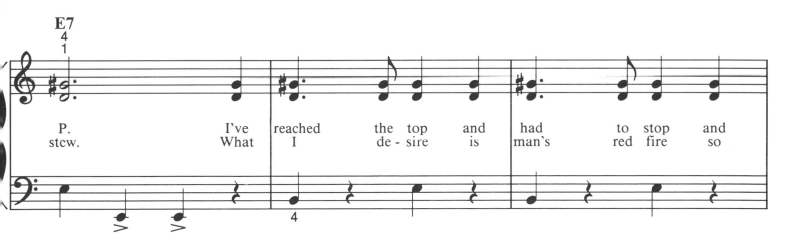

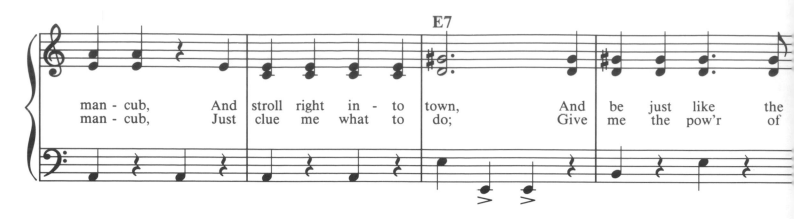

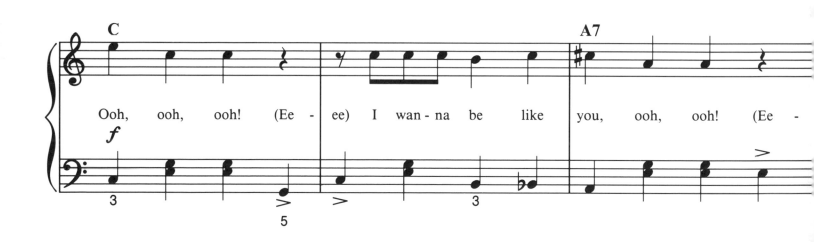

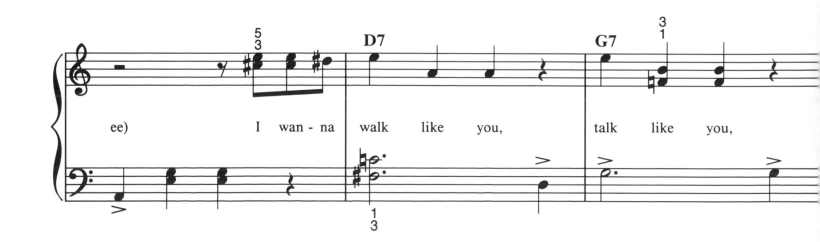

59

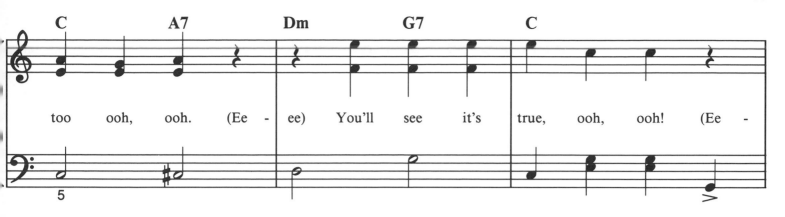

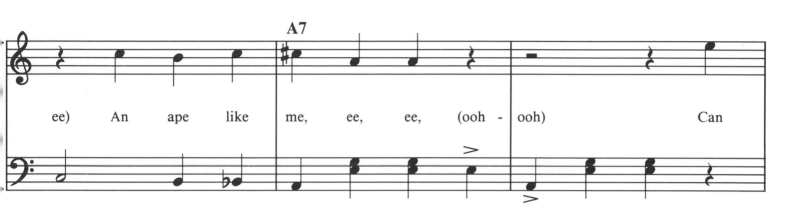

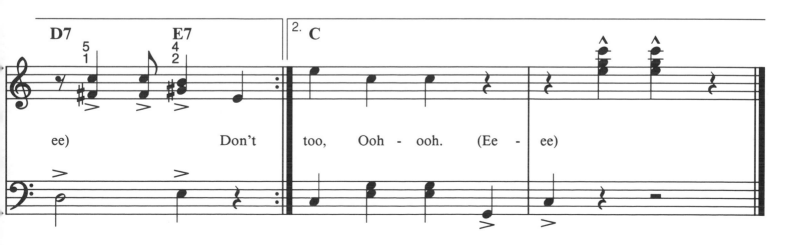

# I WONDER
## (From Walt Disney's "SLEEPING BEAUTY")

Words by WINSTON HIBLER and TED SEARS
Music by GEORGE BRUNS
(Adapted From Tschaikowsky Theme)

I won - der, eh ____ I won - der, ____

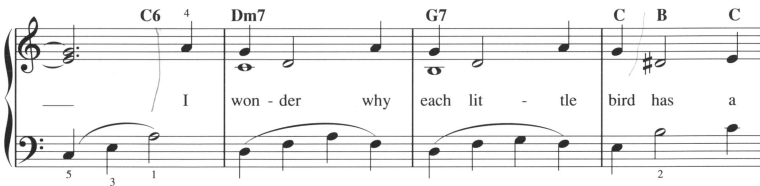

____ I won - der why each lit - tle bird has a

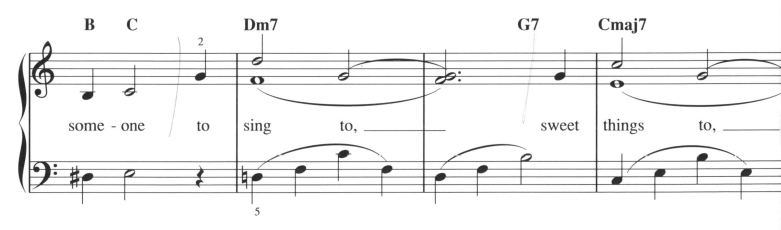

some - one to sing to, ____ sweet things to, ____

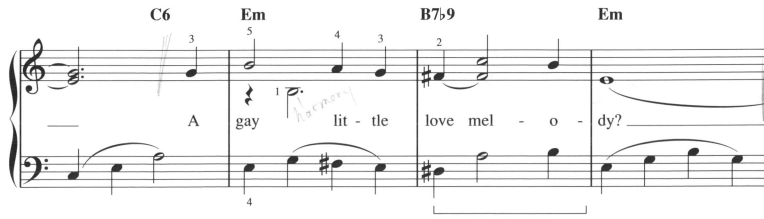

A gay lit - tle love mel - o - dy? ____

61

# I'VE GOT NO STRINGS
## (From Walt Disney's "PINOCCHIO")

Words by NED WASHINGTON
Music by LEIGH HARLINE

Joyfully

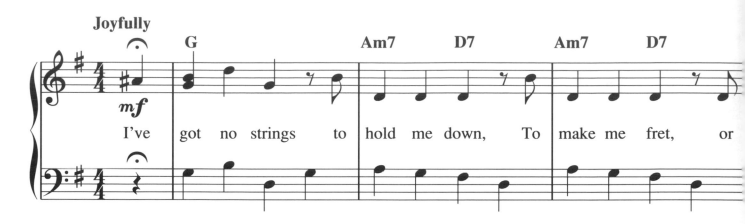

I've got no strings to hold me down, To make me fret, or

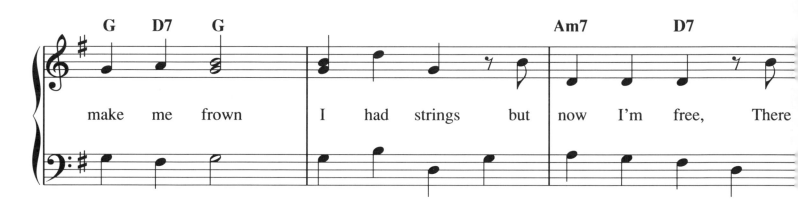

make me frown   I had strings but now I'm free,   There

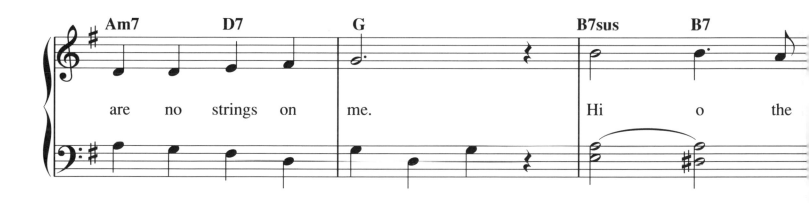

are no strings on me.   Hi   o   the

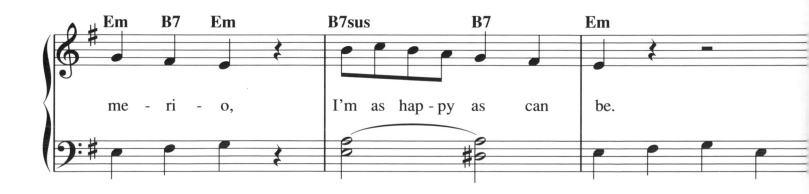

me - ri - o,   I'm as hap-py as can be.

# IT'S A SMALL WORLD

## (Theme From the Disneyland and Walt Disney World Attraction, "IT'S A SMALL WORLD")

Words and Music by RICHARD M. SHERMAN
and ROBERT B. SHERMAN

Brisk March tempo

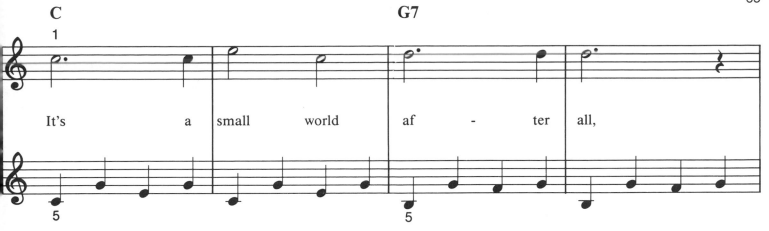

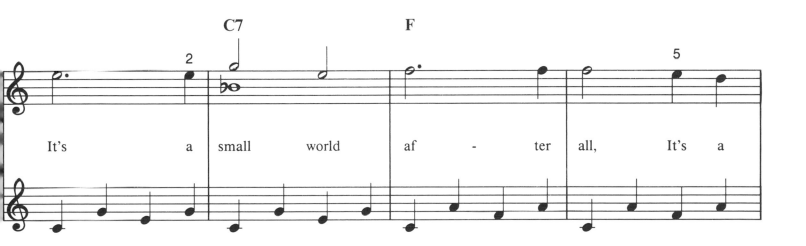

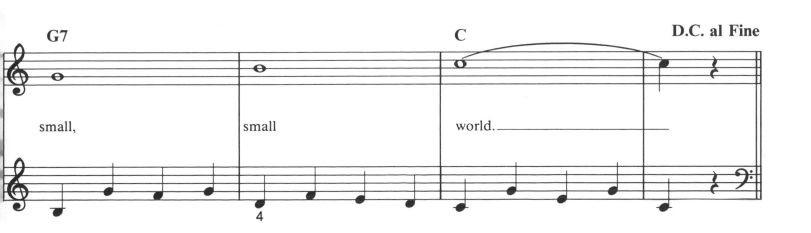

# JOLLY HOLIDAY

Words and Music by RICHARD M. SHERMA
and ROBERT B. SHERMA

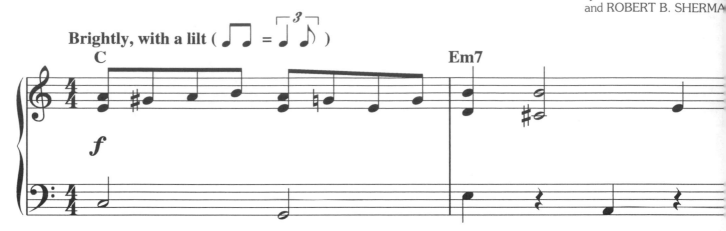

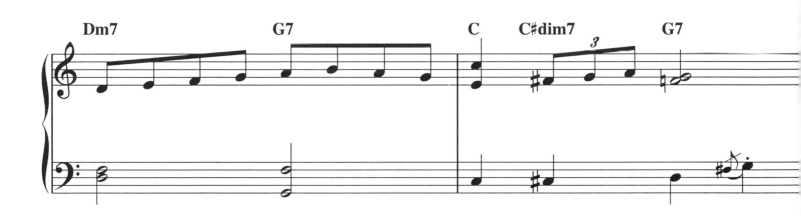

Bert: Ain't it a glo-ri-ous day? Right as a morn-in' in May. I
Now then, what-'d be nice? We'll start with rasp-ber-ry ice, and
Mary Poppins:

feel like I could fly. 'Ave you ev-er seen the
then some cakes and tea. Or-der what you will, there'l
Penguins:

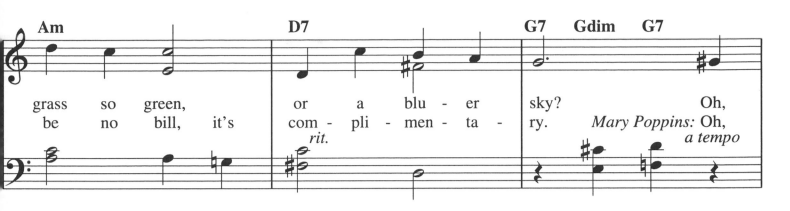

**Am**       **D7**       **G7**   **Gdim**   **G7**

grass so green,    or a blu - er    sky?     Oh,
be no bill, it's    com - pli - men - ta - ry.    *Mary Poppins:* Oh,

*rit.*           *a tempo*

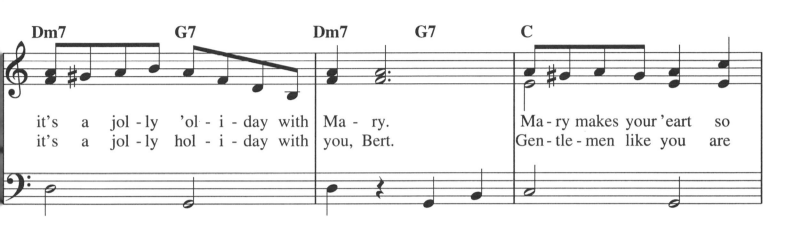

**Dm7**     **G7**      **Dm7**    **G7**      **C**

it's a jol - ly 'ol - i - day with Ma - ry.
it's a jol - ly hol - i - day with you, Bert.

Ma - ry makes your 'eart so
Gen - tle - men like you are

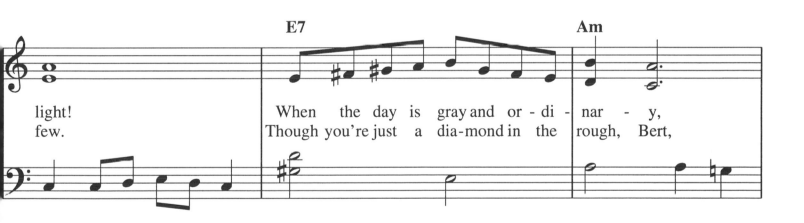

            **E7**            **Am**

light!     When the day is gray and or - di - nar - y,
few.     Though you're just a dia - mond in the rough, Bert,

**D7**           **G7**      **Dm7**      **G7**

Ma - ry makes the sun shine bright! Oh, 'ap - pi - ness is bloom - in' all a -
un - der - neath your blood is blue! You'd nev - er think of press - ing your ad -

68

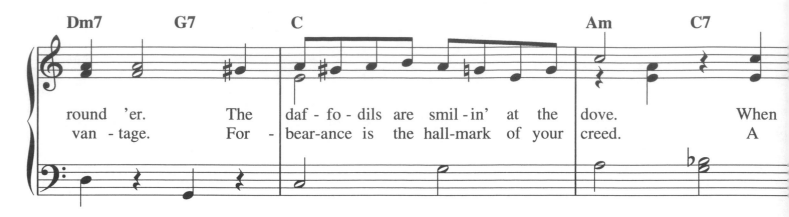

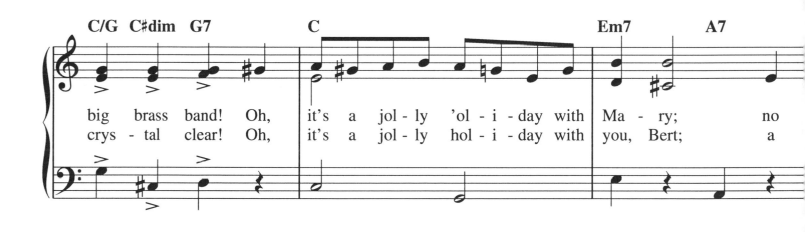

# KISS THE GIRL

## (From Walt Disney's "THE LITTLE MERMAID")

Lyrics by HOWARD ASHMAN
Music by ALAN MENKEN

There you see her

sit-ting there a-cross the way

way

She don't got a lot to say,

but there's some - thing a - bout her. And you

don't know why, __ but you're dy - ing to try. You wan-na kiss the girl.

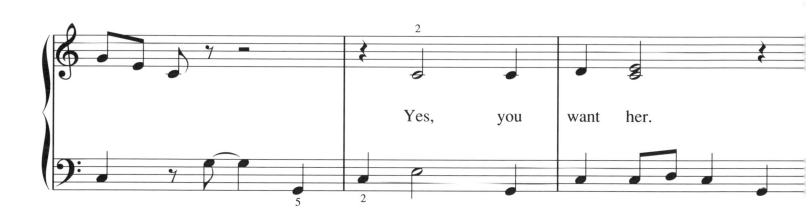

Yes, you want her.

Look at her, you know you do. Pos - si -ble she wants you, too. __

There is one way to ask her. It don't

take a word, __ not a sin - gle word, _ go on and kiss the girl.

Sha la la la la la, my oh my, __ Look like the

boy too shy. __ Ain't gon - na kiss the girl. Sha la la la la la,

ain't that sad. __ Ain't it a shame, too bad. __ He gon - na miss the girl. __

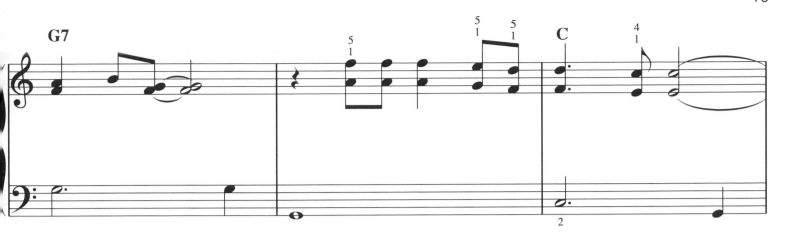

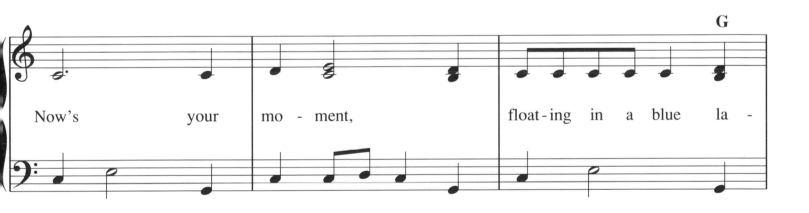

Now's your mo - ment, float-ing in a blue la -

goon. Boy, you bet - ter do it soon, no time will be

bet - ter.     She don't say a word _ and she

won't say a word un - til you  kiss the girl.

1. Sha la la la la la, don't be scared. _ You got the mood pre-pared, _ go on and
2. Sha la la la la la, float a - long. __ And lis - ten to the song, _ the song say

kiss the girl.    Sha la la la la la, don't stop now. _ Don't try to
kiss the girl.    Sha la la la la the mu - sic play. _ Do what the

# LAVENDER BLUE (DILLY, DILLY)
## (From Walt Disney's "SO DEAR TO MY HEART")

Words by LARRY MOREY
Music by ELIOT DANIEL

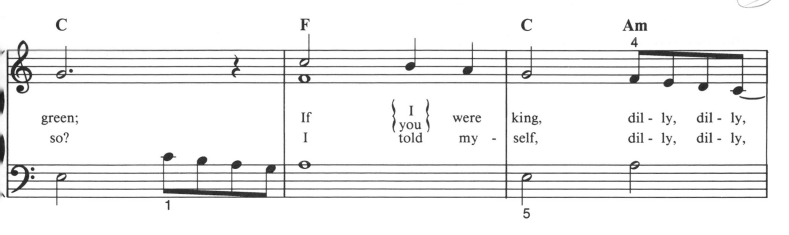

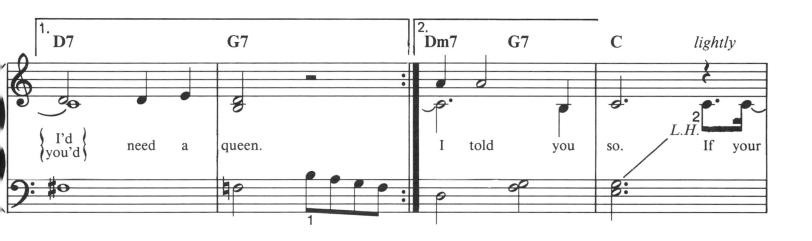

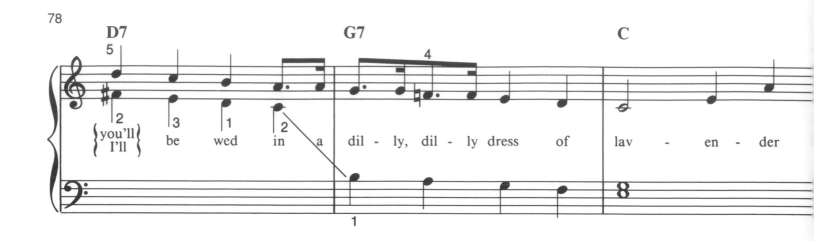

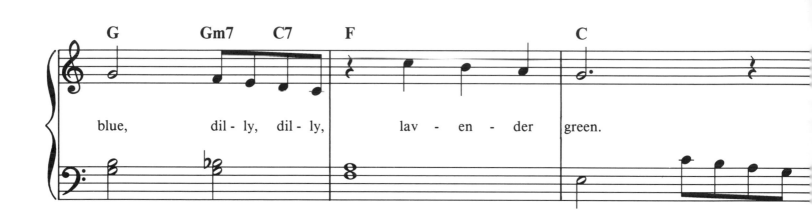

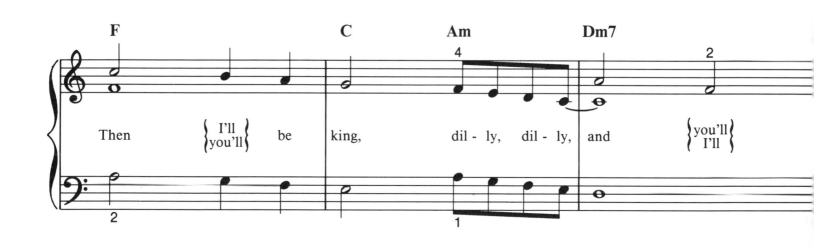

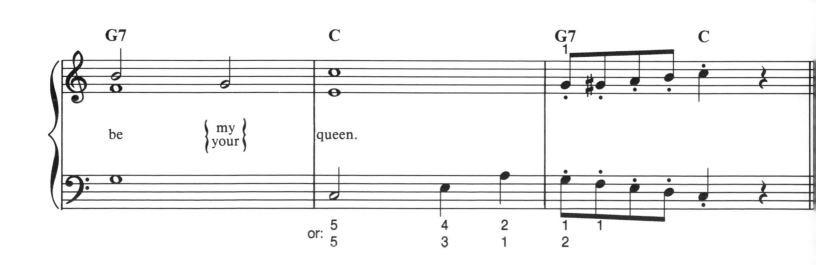

# LITTLE APRIL SHOWER

### (From Walt Disney's "BAMBI")

Words by LARRY MOREY
Music by FRANK CHURCHILL

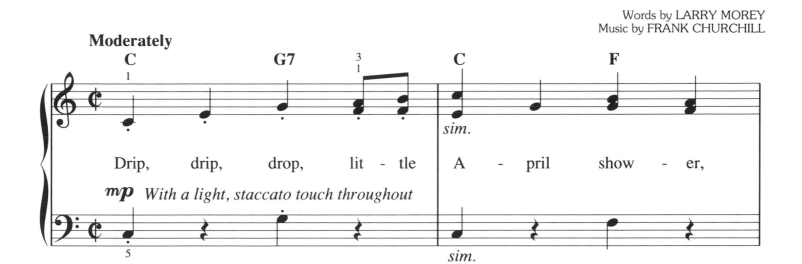

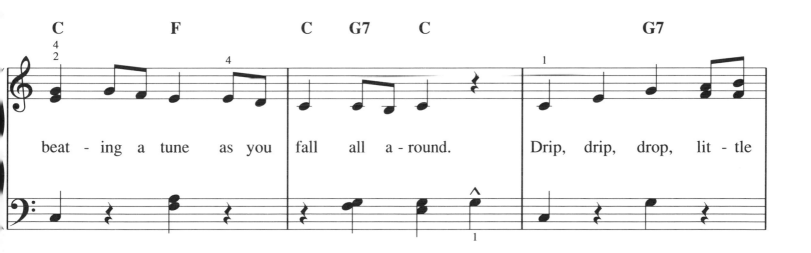

Drip, drip, drop, when the sky is cloud - y your pret - ty mu - sic can

bright - en the day. Drip, drip, drop, when the sun says "How - dy"

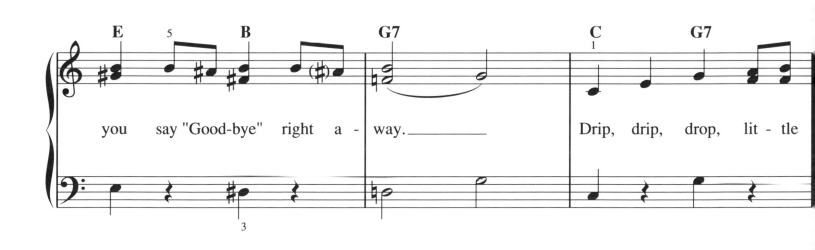

you say "Good-bye" right a - way._____ Drip, drip, drop, lit - tle

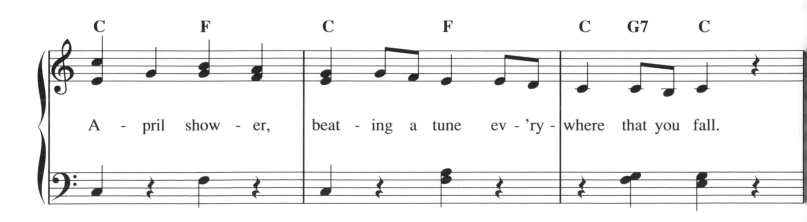

A - pril show - er, beat - ing a tune ev - 'ry - where that you fall.

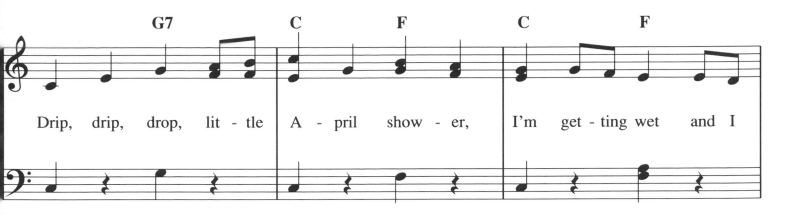

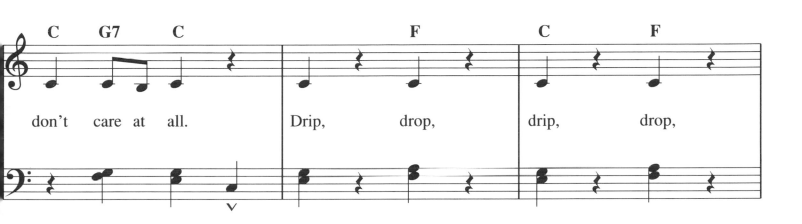

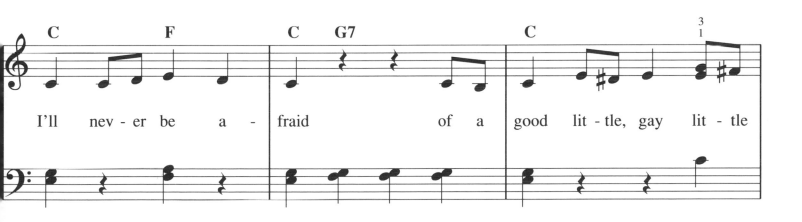

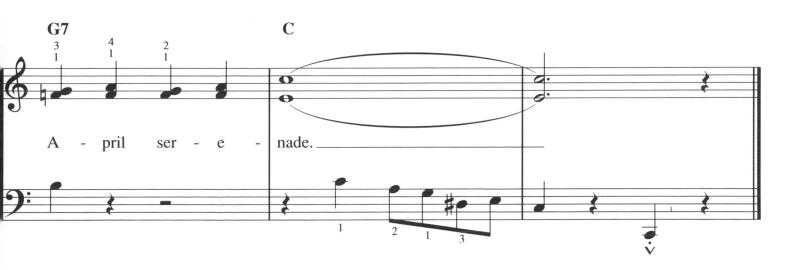

# LET'S GO FLY A KITE
## (From Walt Disney's "MARY POPPINS")

Words and Music by RICHARD M. SHERMAN
and ROBERT B. SHERMAN

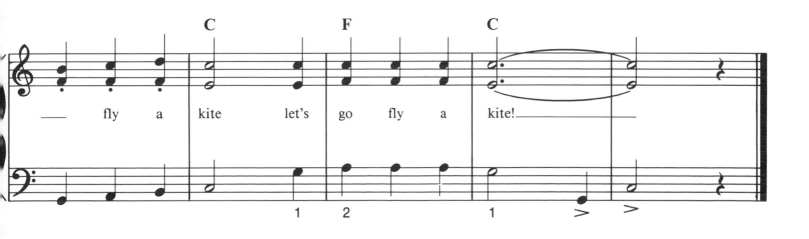

# LOVE IS A SONG
(From Walt Disney's "BAMBI")

Words by LARRY MORE
Music by FRANK CHURCHIL

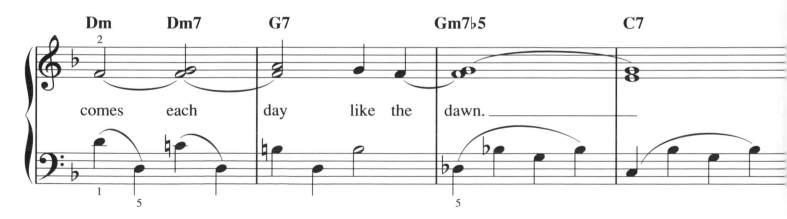

85

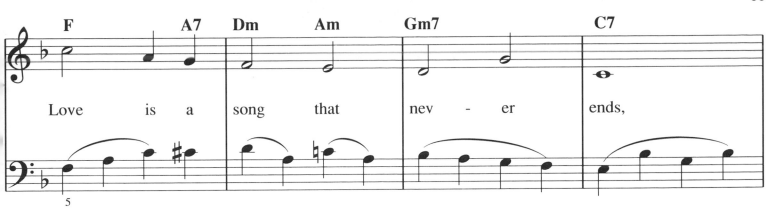

Love is a    song that    nev - er    ends,

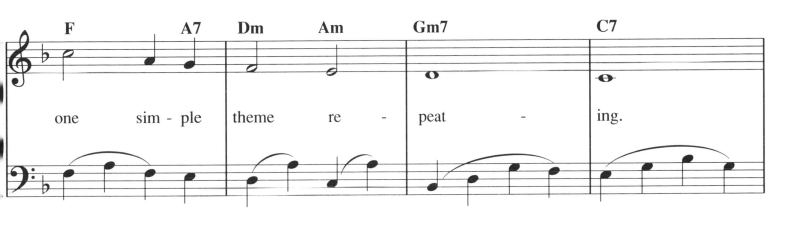

one    sim - ple    theme    re -    peat -    ing.

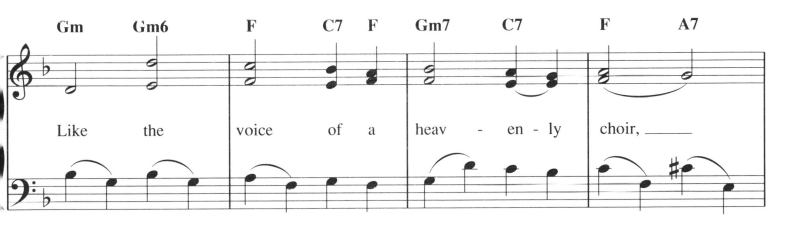

Like    the    voice    of    a    heav - en - ly    choir, _____

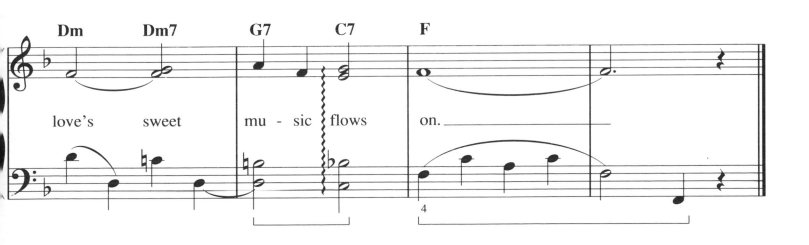

love's    sweet    mu - sic flows    on. _____

# MICKEY MOUSE ALMA MATER

## (From Walt Disney's TV Series "THE MICKEY MOUSE CLUB")

Words and Music b
JIMMIE DOD

# MICKEY MOUSE MARCH
## (From Walt Disney's TV Series "THE MICKEY MOUSE CLUB")

Words and Music by
JIMMIE DODD

**Brightly**

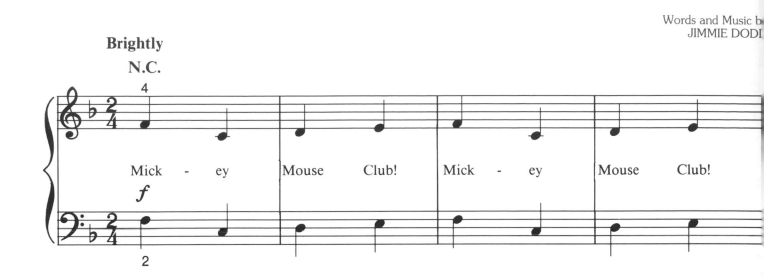

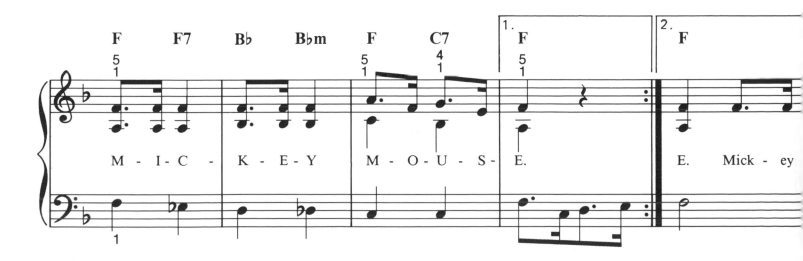

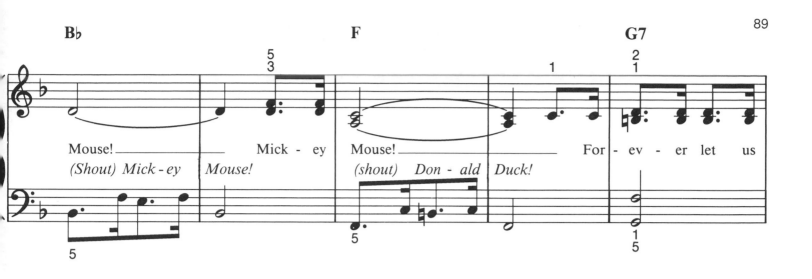

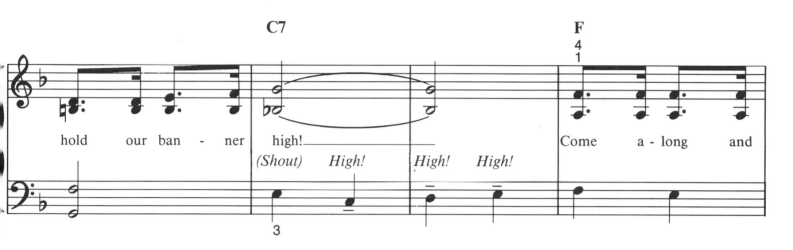

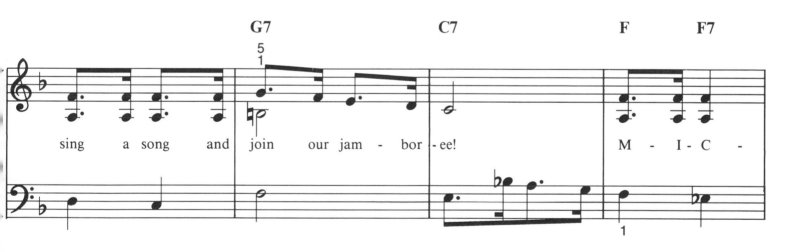

for Oct. 14

# ONCE UPON A DREAM

### (From Walt Disney's "SLEEPING BEAUTY")

Words and Adaptation of Music by SAMMY FAIN
and JACK LAWRENCE
based on Sleeping Beauty Theme

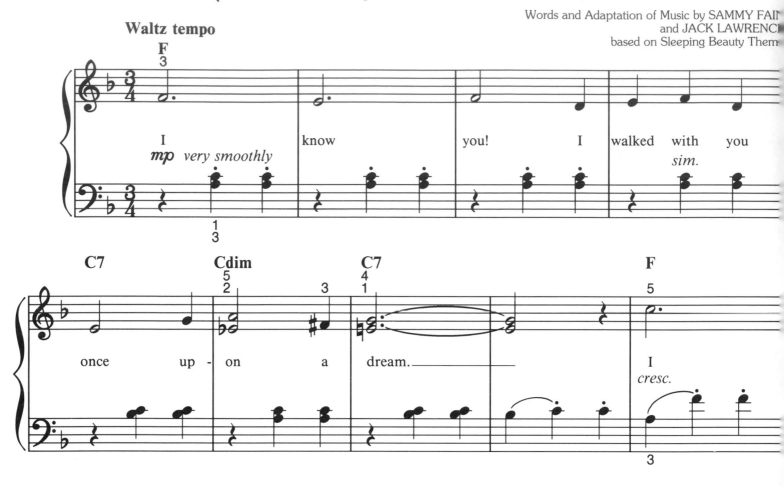

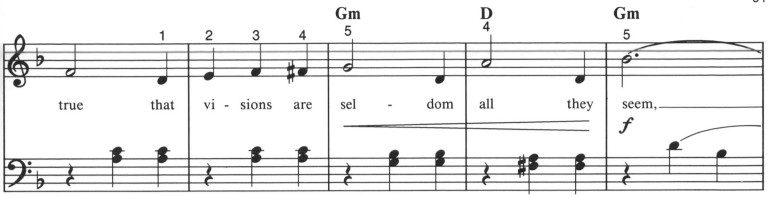

true that vi - sions are sel - dom all they seem,

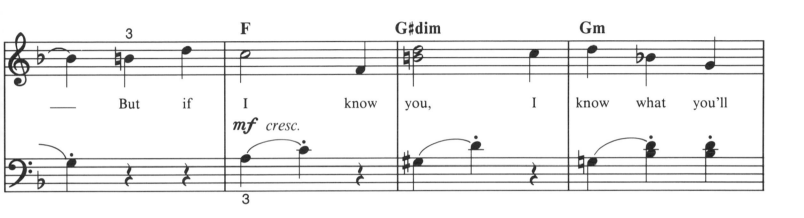

But if I know you, I know what you'll

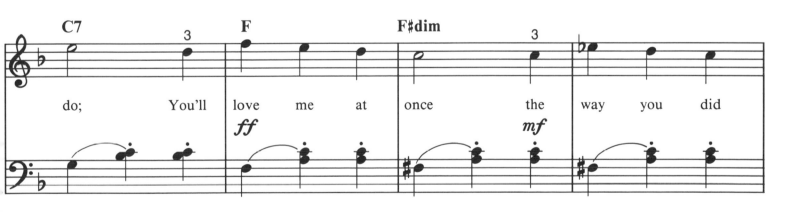

do; You'll love me at once the way you did

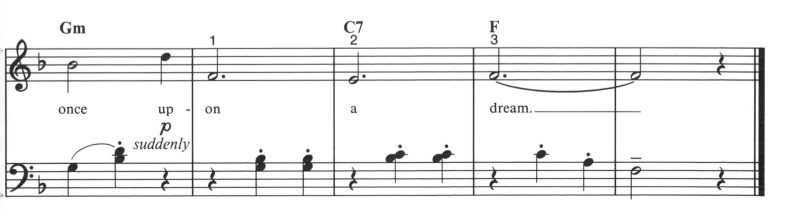

once up - on a dream.

# ONE SONG

## (From Walt Disney's "SNOW WHITE AND THE SEVEN DWARFS")

Words by LARRY MOREY
Music by FRANK CHURCHILL

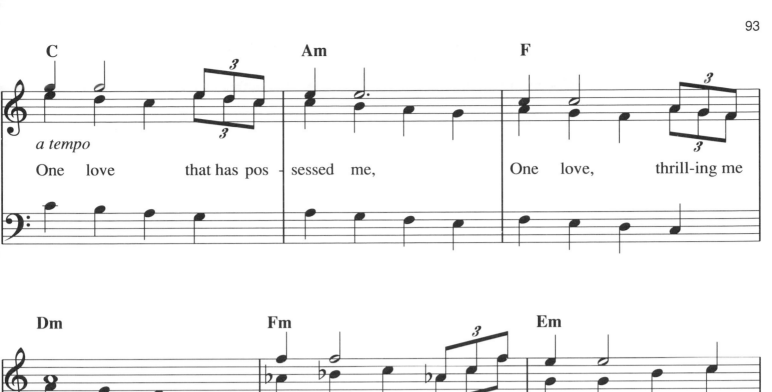

One love that has pos - sessed me, One love, thrill-ing me

through, One song, my heart keeps sing - ing of

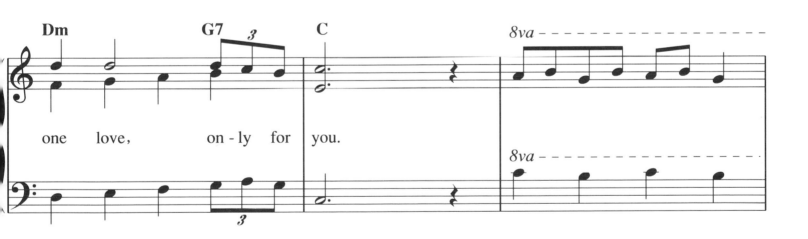

one love, on - ly for you.

# PART OF YOUR WORLD
## (From Walt Disney's "THE LITTLE MERMAID")

Lyrics by HOWARD ASHMAN
Music by ALAN MENKEN

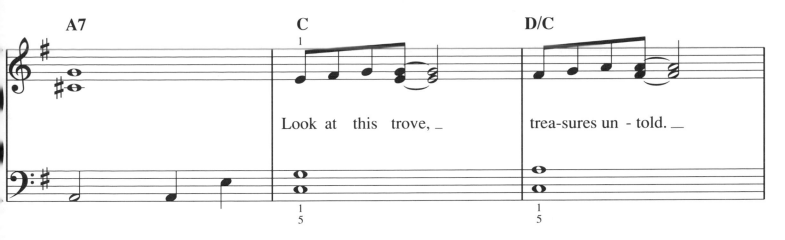

Look at this trove, _ trea-sures un - told. _

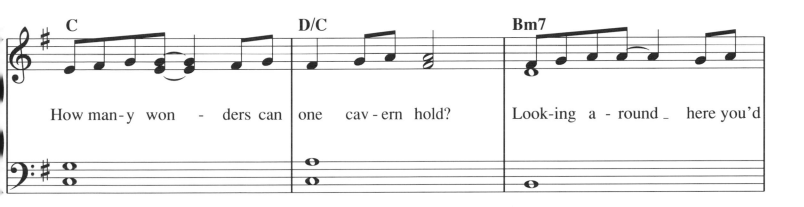

How man-y won - ders can one cav-ern hold? Look-ing a - round _ here you'd

think, sure, she's got ev - 'ry -thing. _ I've got

gad - gets and giz - mos a - plen-ty. _ I've got who - zits and what-zits ga -

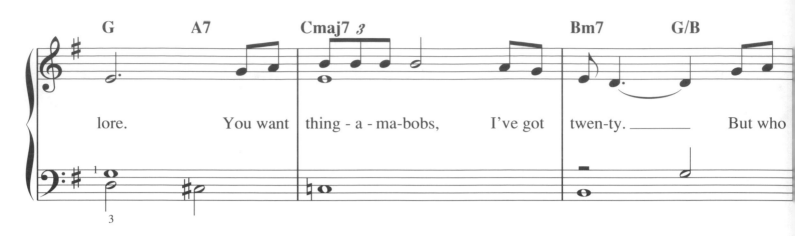

lore.        You want | thing - a - ma-bobs,        I've got | twen-ty. ____        But who

cares?        No big | deal.        I want | more.

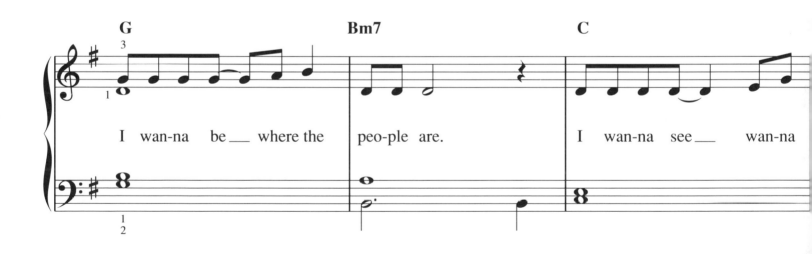

I   wan-na    be __ where the | peo-ple   are.        | I   wan-na   see __      wan-na

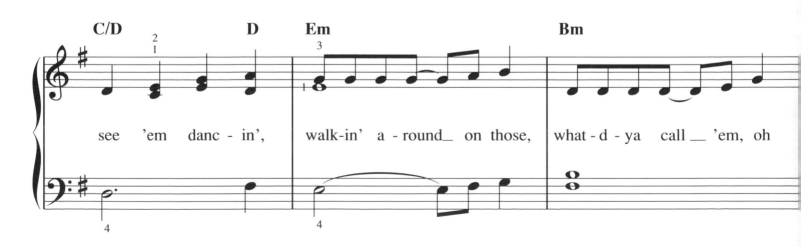

see  'em   danc - in', | walk-in'  a - round_ on those, | what - d - ya   call __ 'em, oh

stay all day in the sun. Wan - der - in' free, wish I could

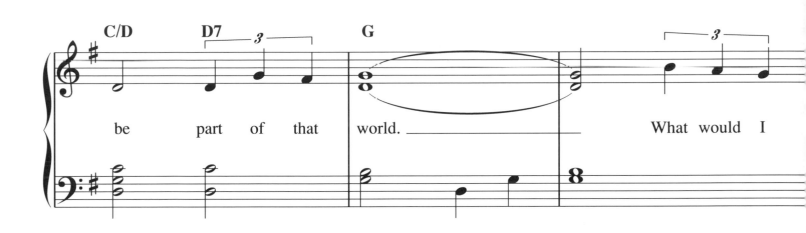

be part of that world. _____ What would I

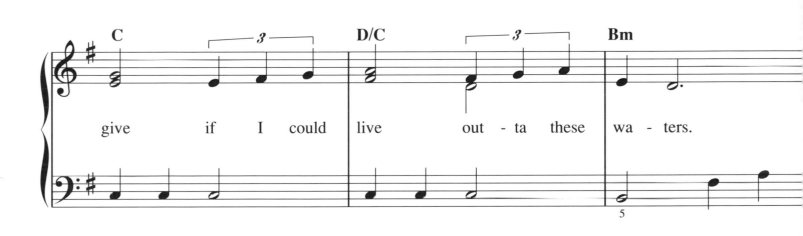

give if I could live out - ta these wa - ters.

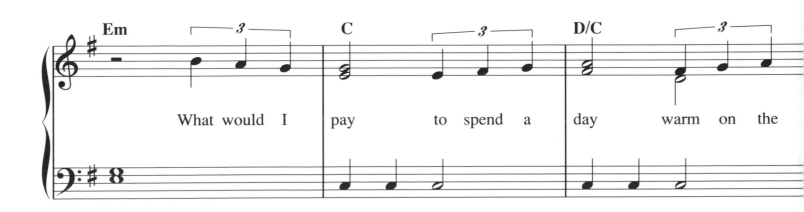

What would I pay to spend a day warm on the

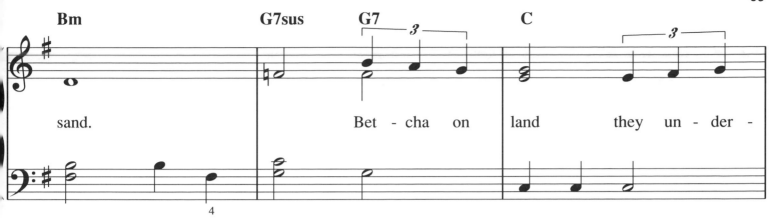

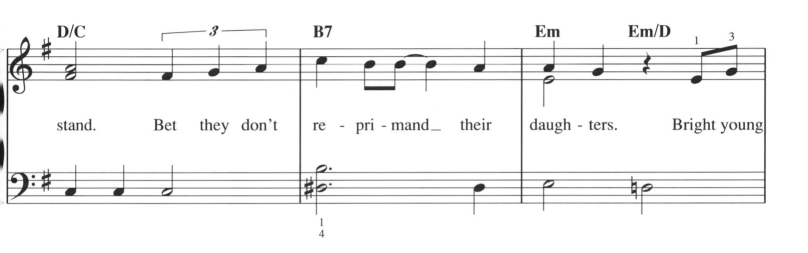

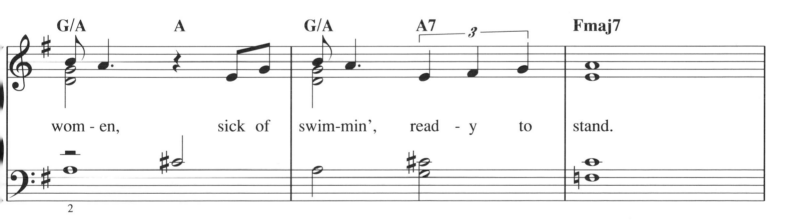

100

Ask 'em my ques - tions and get some an - swers. What's a fire _____ and

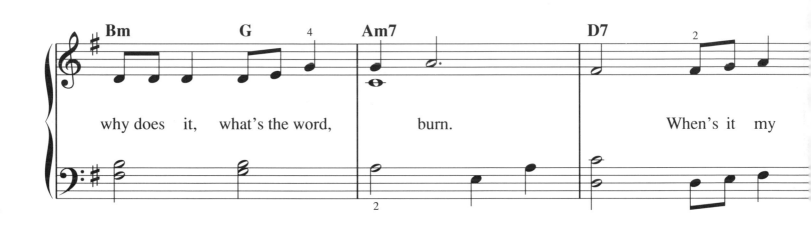

why does it, what's the word, burn. When's it my

turn? Would-n't I love, love to ex - plore that shore up a -

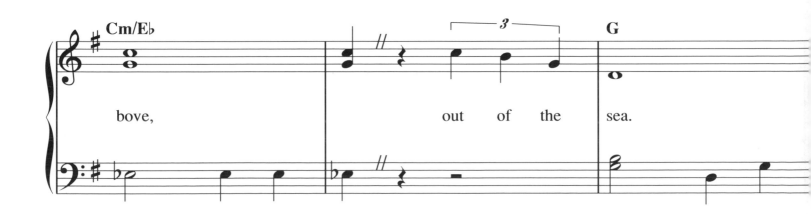

bove, out of the sea.

# SALUDOS AMIGOS
(From Walt Disney's "THE THREE CABALLEROS")

Words by NED WASHINGTO
Music by CHARLES WOLCOT

**With spirit, in 2 ( ♩ = 1 beat )**

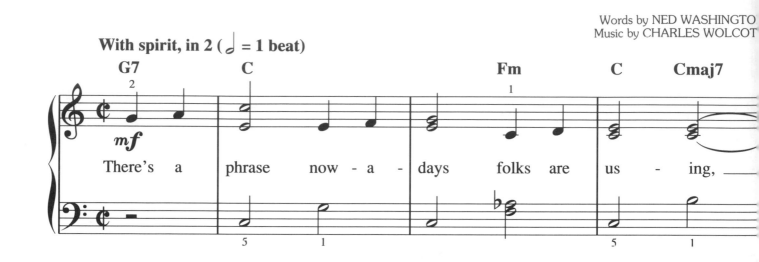

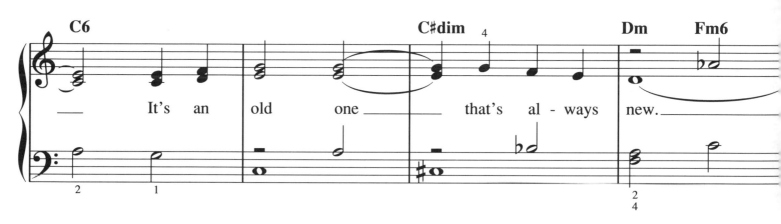

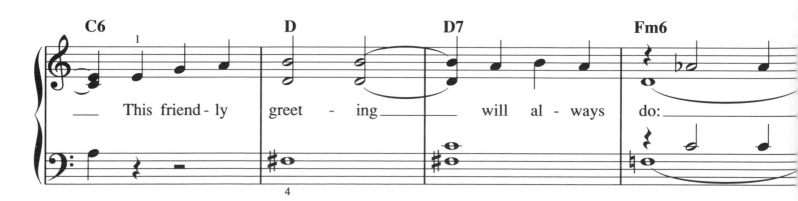

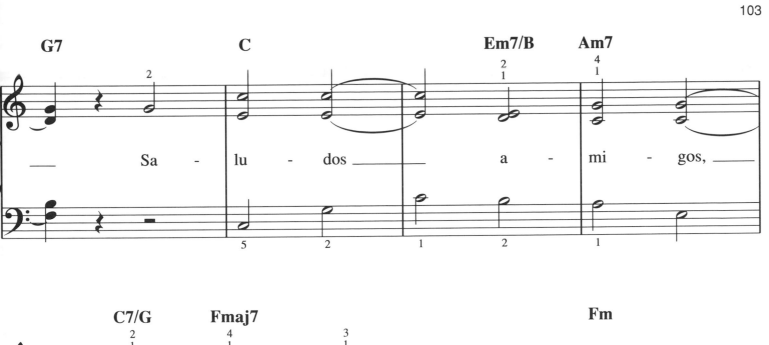

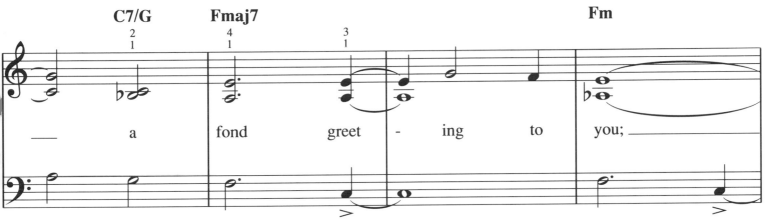

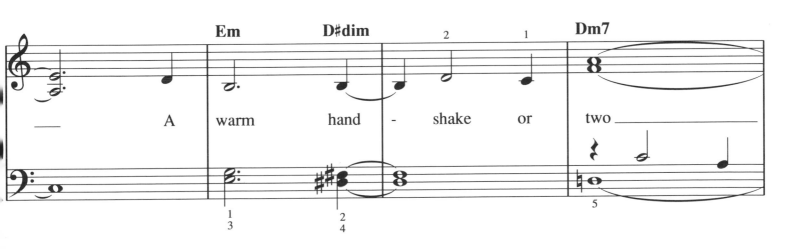

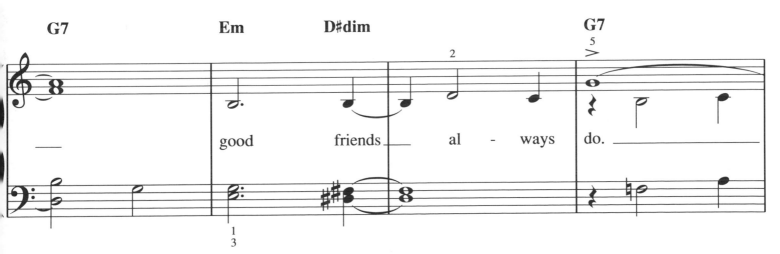

104

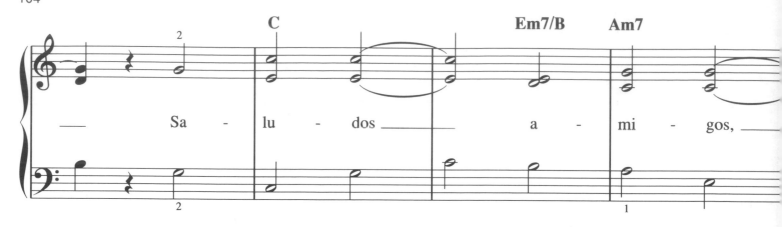

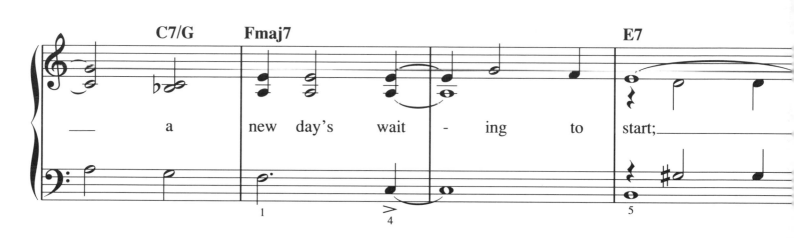

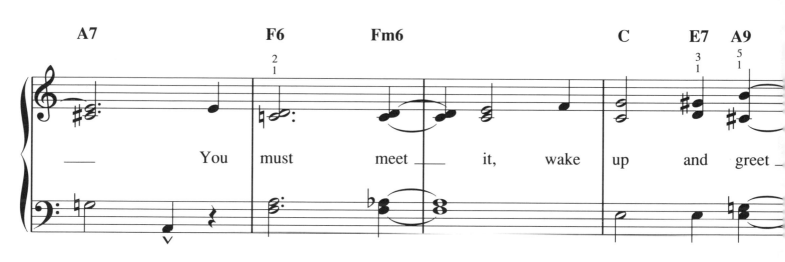

# THE SECOND STAR TO THE RIGHT

(From Walt Disney's "PETER PAN")

Words by SAMMY CAHN
Music by SAMMY FAIN

**Slowly, with expression**

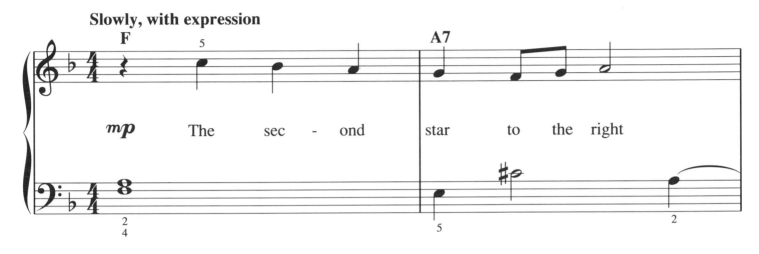

The sec - ond star to the right

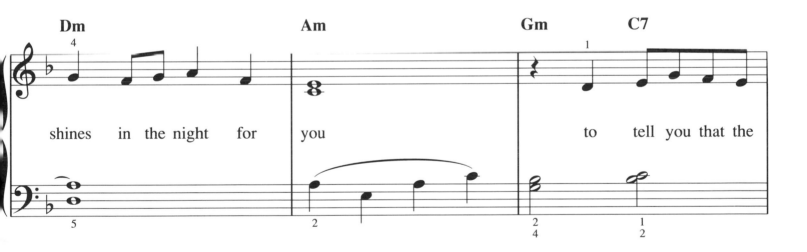

shines in the night for you to tell you that the

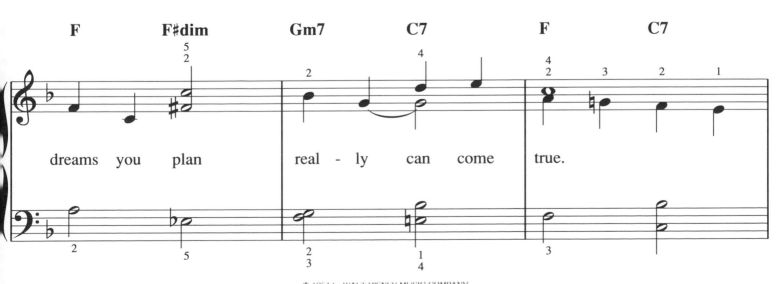

dreams you plan real - ly can come true.

106

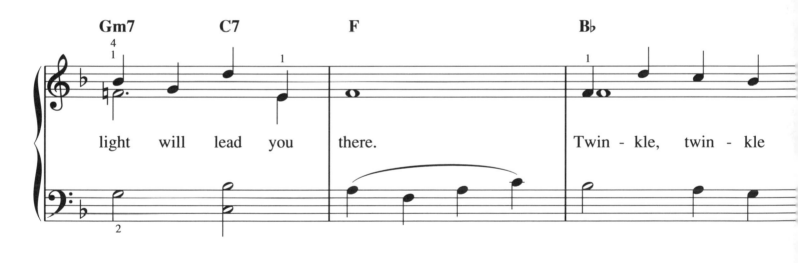

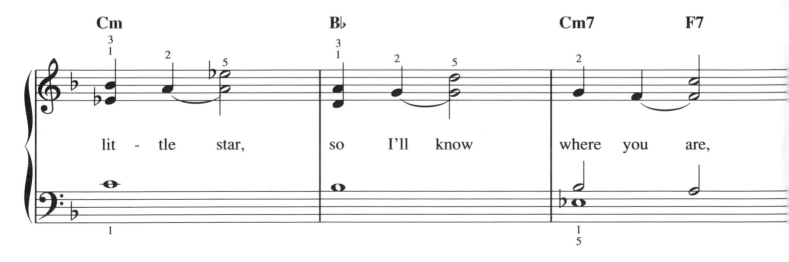

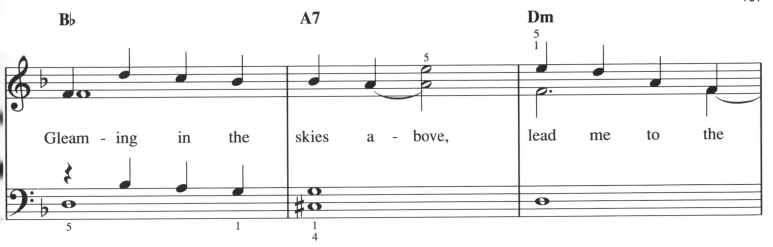

Gleam - ing in the skies a - bove, lead me to the

*Slower*       *a tempo*

one who loves me. And when you bring him my way,

each time we say, "Good - night," we'll thank the lit - tle

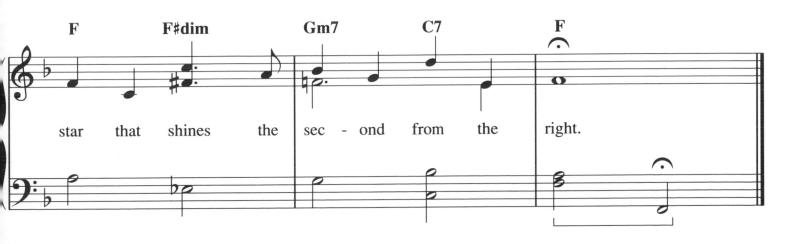

star that shines the sec - ond from the right.

# THE SIAMESE CAT SONG

### (From Walt Disney's "LADY AND THE TRAMP")

Words and Music by PEGGY LEE
and SONNY BURKE

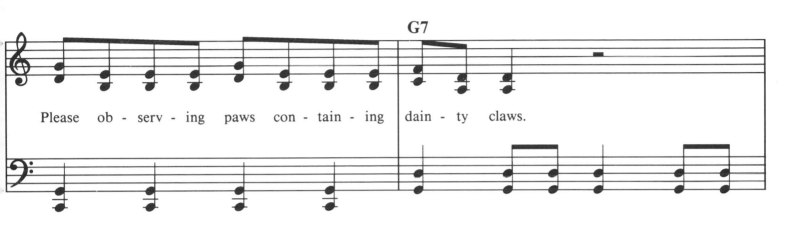

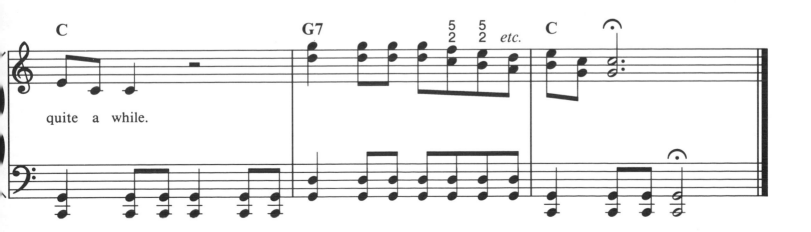

# SO THIS IS LOVE
## (From Walt Disney's "CINDERELLA")

Words and Music by MACK DAVID
AL HOFFMAN and JERRY LIVINGSTON

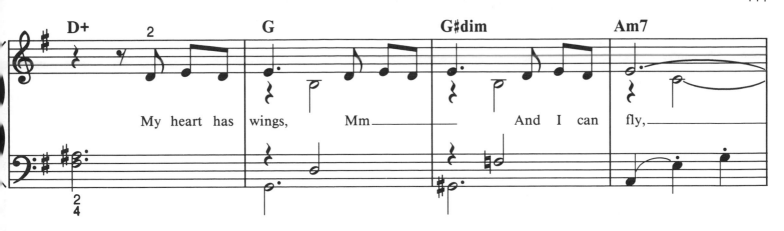

My heart has wings, Mm_____ And I can fly,_____

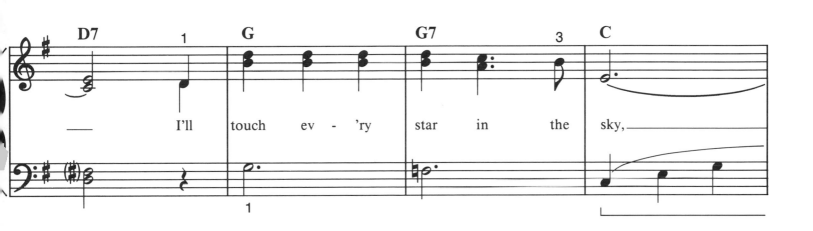

_____ I'll touch ev - 'ry star in the sky,_____

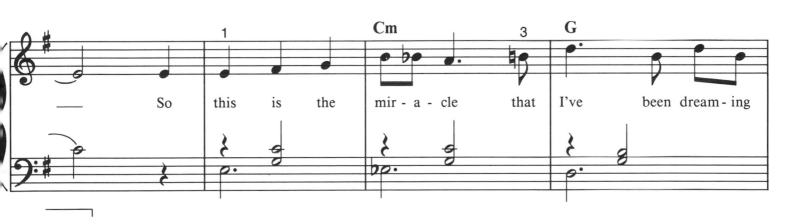

_____ So this is the mir - a - cle that I've been dream - ing

of, Mm_____ Mm_____ So this is love._____

# SOME DAY MY PRINCE WILL COME

(From Walt Disney's "SNOW WHITE AND THE SEVEN DWARFS")

Words by LARRY MOREY
Music by FRANK CHURCHILL

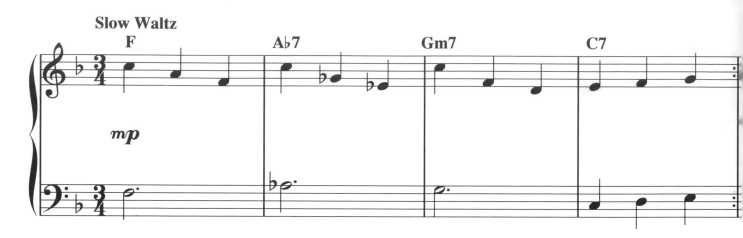

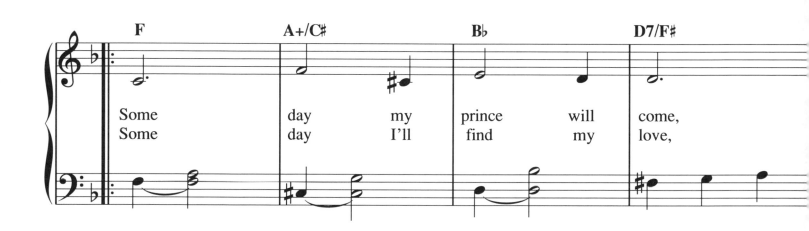

Some day my prince will come,
Some day I'll find my love,

Some day I'll find my love and how
Some one to call my own, and I'll

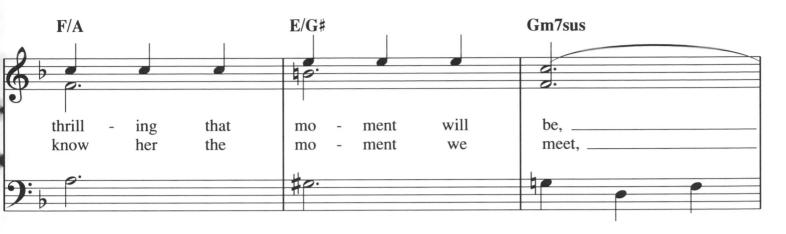

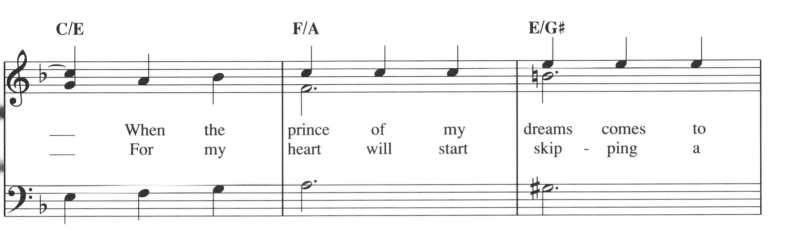

kiss  or  two Though he's
long - ing  to Though she's  far  a - way  I'll

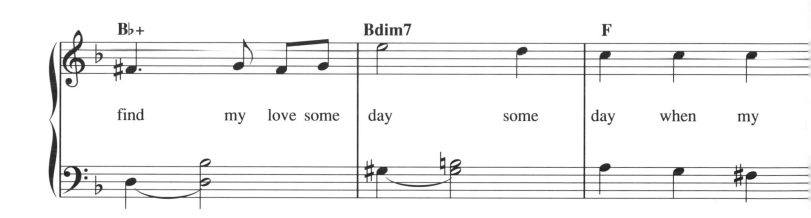

find  my love some  day    some  day  when  my

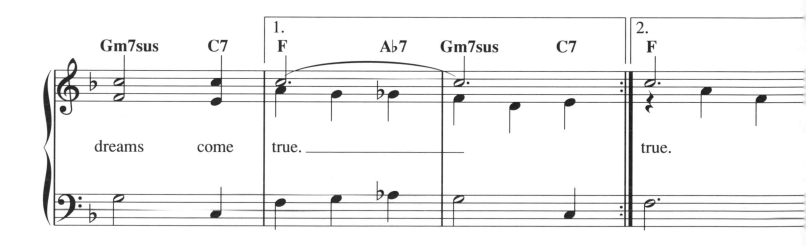

dreams  come  true. _____         true.

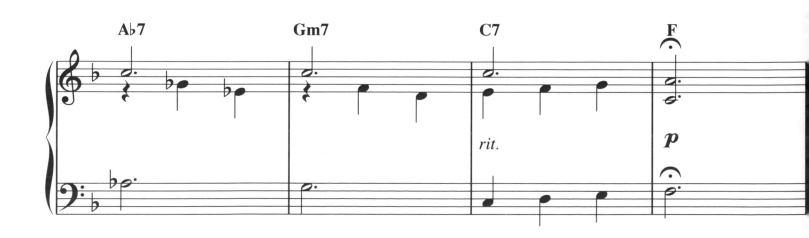

# SUPERCALIFRAGILISTICEXPIALIDOCIOUS

## (From Walt Disney's "MARY POPPINS")

Words and Music by RICHARD M. SHERMAN
and ROBERT B. SHERMAN

Brightly

Um did-dle did-dle did-dle um did-dle ay!

Um did-dle did-dle did-dle um did-dle ay!

1.2.Su - per - cal - i - frag - il - is - tic - ex - pi - al - i - do - cious!
3.Su - per - cal - i - frag - il - is - tic - ex - pi - al - i - do - cious!

E - ven though the sound of it is some - thing quite a - tro - cious,
Su - per - cal - i - frag - il - is - tic - ex - pi - al - i - do - cious,

if you say it loud e- nough you'll al - ways sound pre - co - cious:
Su - per- cal - i - frag - il - is - tic - ex - pi - al - i - do - cious,

Su - per - cal - i - frag - il - is - tic - ex - pi - al - i - do - cious!
Su - per - cal - i - frag - il - is - tic - ex - pi - al - i - do - cious!

L.H.
Um did - dle did - dle did - dle um did - dle ay! Um did - dle did - dle did - dle

um did - dle ay! {Be - cause I was a - fraid to speak when I was just a
{So when the cat has got your tongue there's no need for dis -

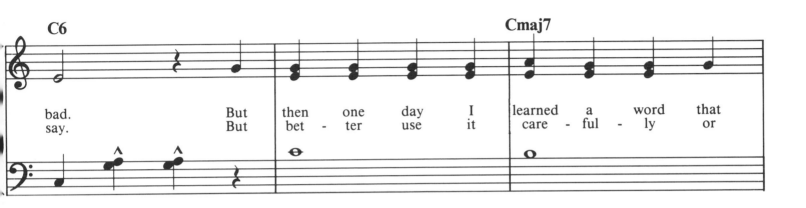

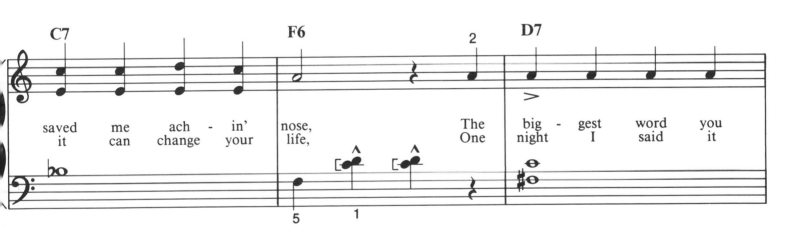

# SOMEONE'S WAITING FOR YOU

(From Walt Disney's "THE RESCUERS")

Words by CAROL CONNORS and AYN ROBBIN
Music by SAMMY FAI

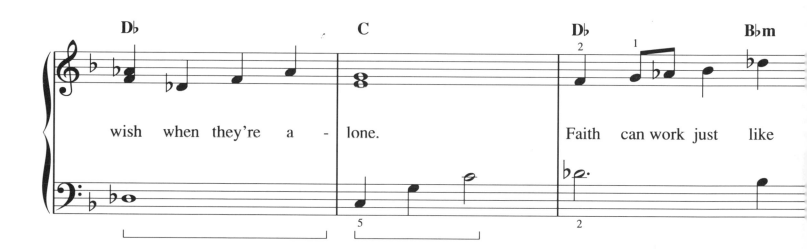

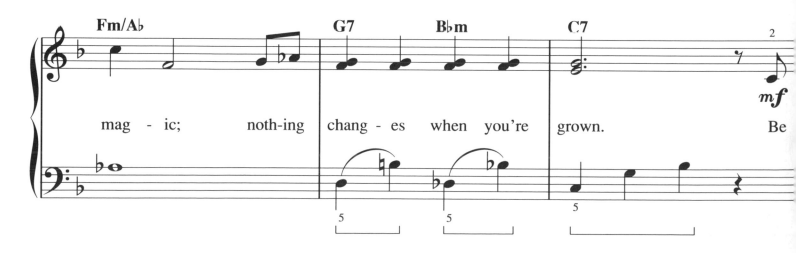

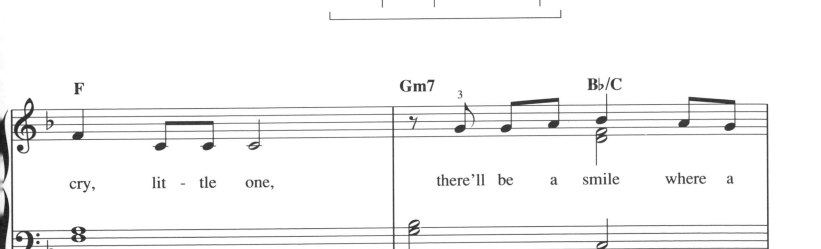

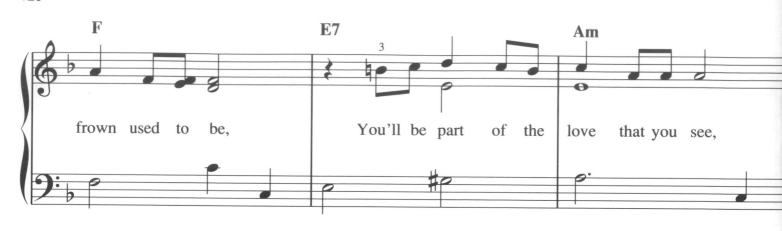

frown used to be, You'll be part of the love that you see,

some-one's wait-ing for you. _____ Al - ways

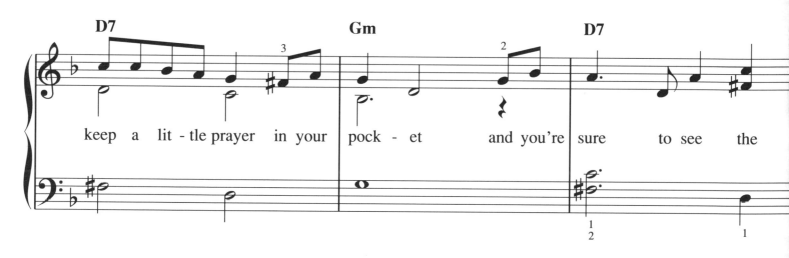

keep a lit - tle prayer in your pock - et and you're sure to see the

light. Soon there'll be joy and hap - pi - ness and

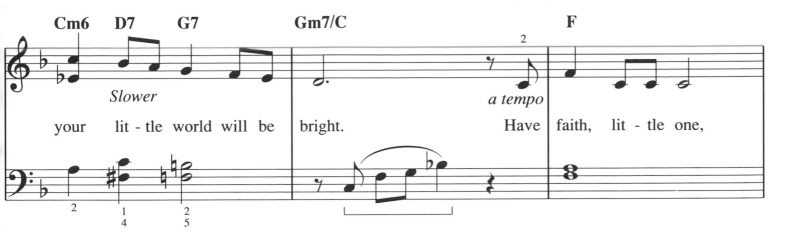

your lit - tle world will be bright. Have faith, lit - tle one,

'til your hopes and your wish - es come true

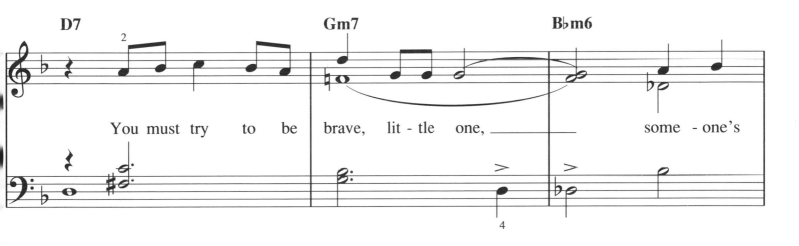

You must try to be brave, lit - tle one, \_\_\_\_\_ some - one's

wait - ing to love you. \_\_\_\_\_

# A SPOONFUL OF SUGAR

## (From Walt Disney's "MARY POPPINS")

Words and Music by RICHARD M. SHERMAN
and ROBERT B. SHERMAN

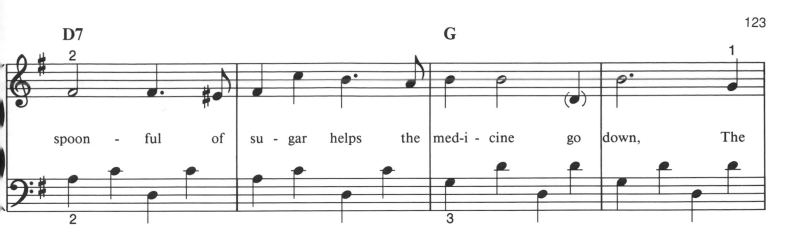

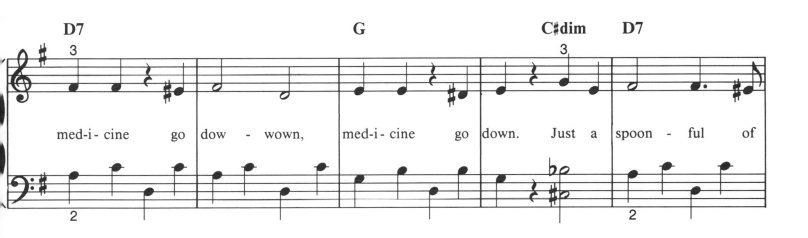

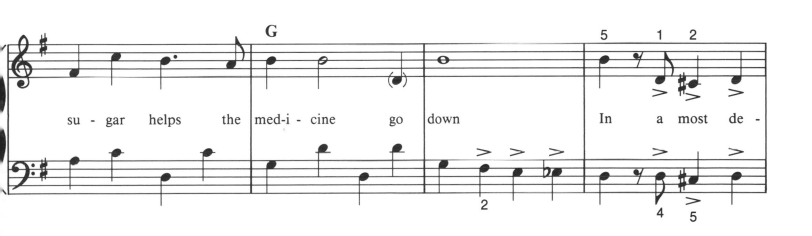

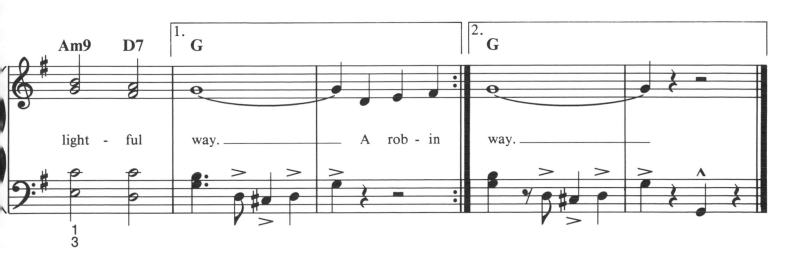

# THE TIKI TIKI TIKI ROOM

(From the Disneyland and Walt Disney World Attraction, "THE ENCHANTED TIKI ROOM")

Words and Music by RICHARD M. SHERMAN
and ROBERT B. SHERMAN

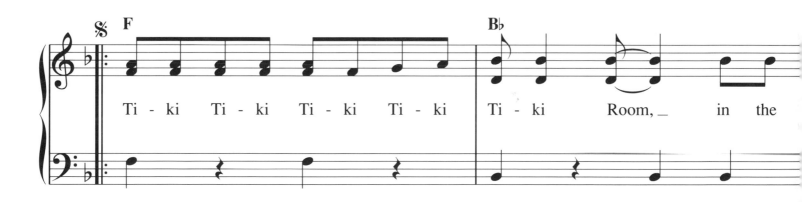

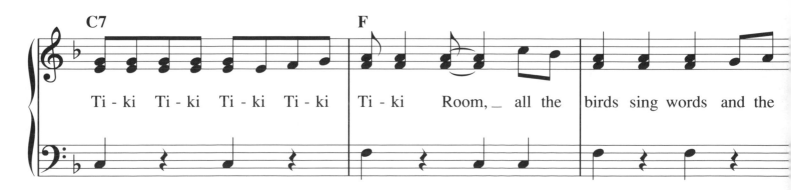

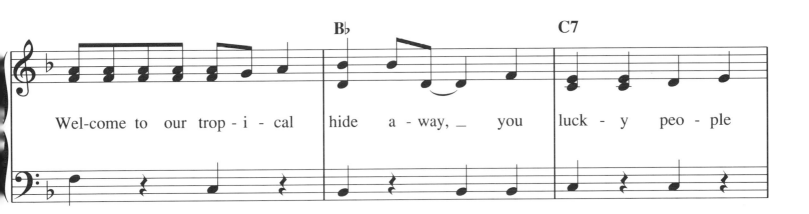

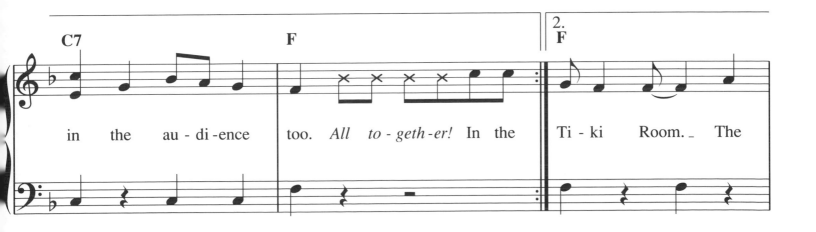

126

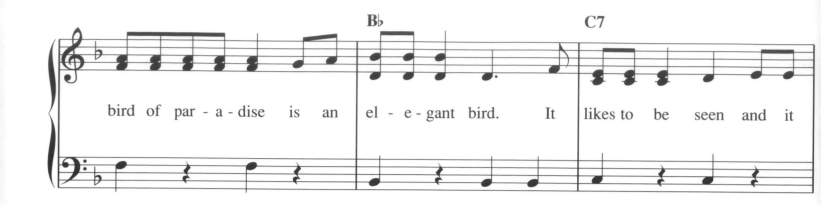

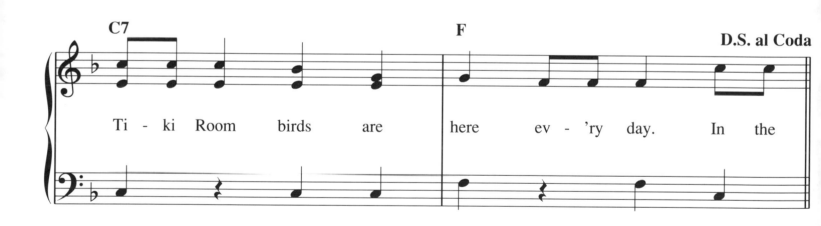

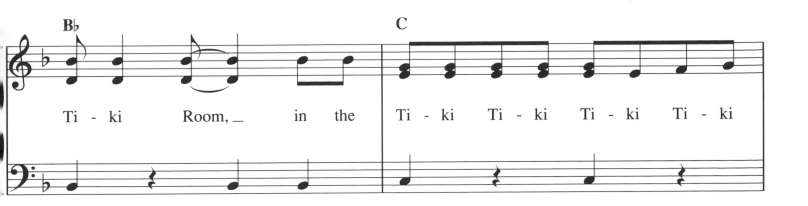

Ti - ki    Room, __    in the    Ti - ki  Ti - ki  Ti - ki  Ti - ki

Ti - ki    Room, __    all the    birds    sing    words    and the

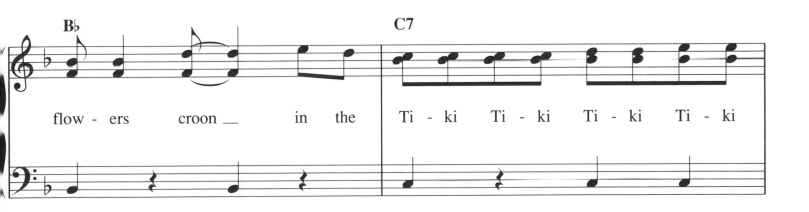

flow - ers    croon __    in the    Ti - ki  Ti - ki  Ti - ki  Ti - ki

Ti - ki    Room. __

# UNDER THE SEA
## (From Walt Disney's "THE LITTLE MERMAID")

Lyrics by HOWARD ASHMAN
Music by ALAN MENKEN

129

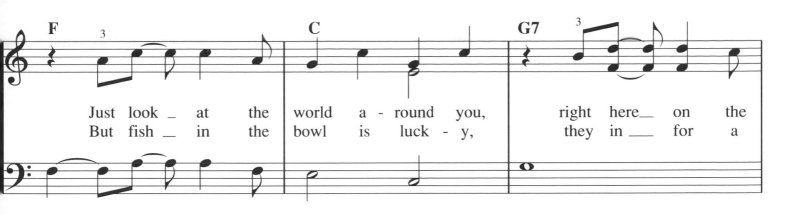

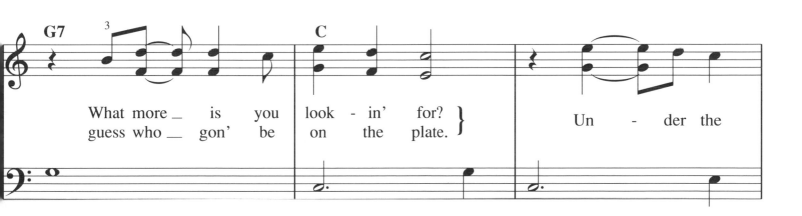

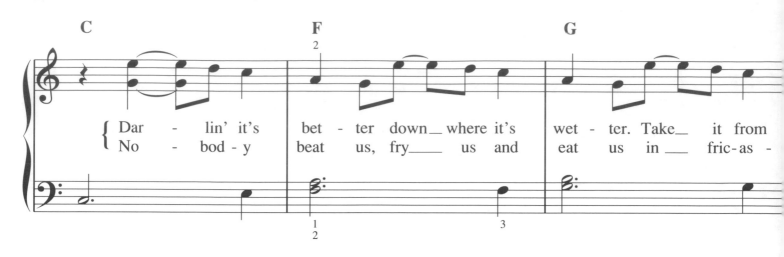

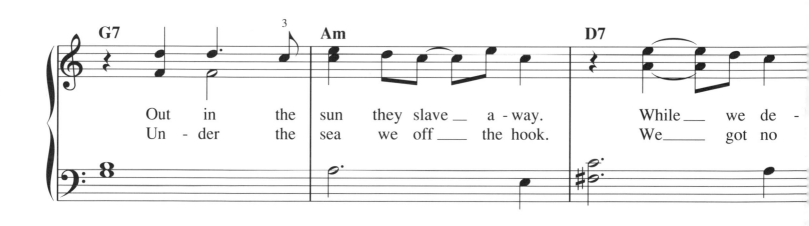

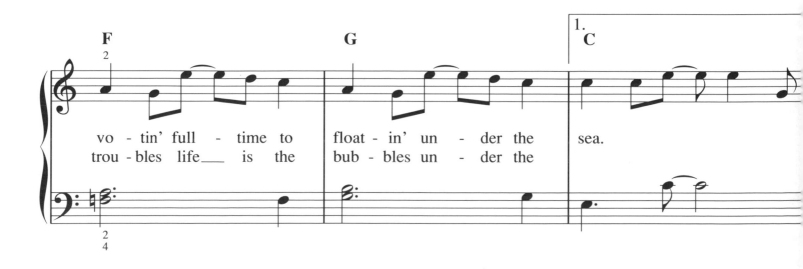

sea.              Un  -  der  the     sea.

Since  life     is    sweet here we ____ got the     beat here nat - u - ral -

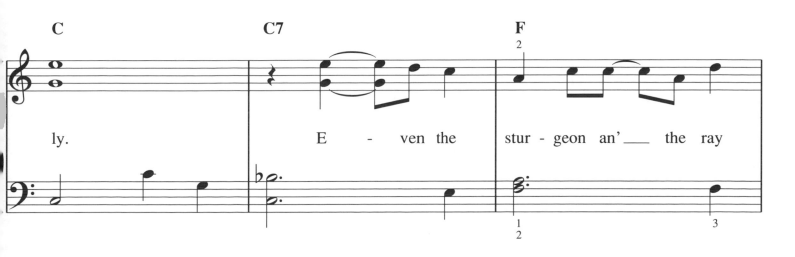

ly.               E   -  ven the    stur - geon an' ____ the ray

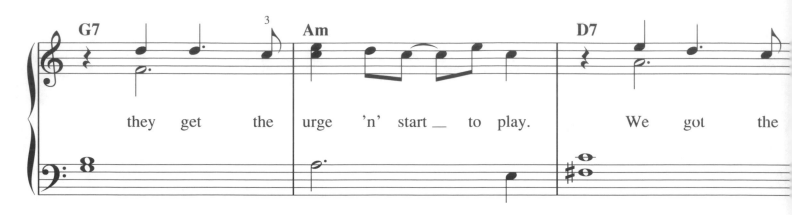

they get the urge 'n' start — to play. We got the

spir - it, you — got to hear it un - der the sea.

The newt play the flute. The carp play the harp. The

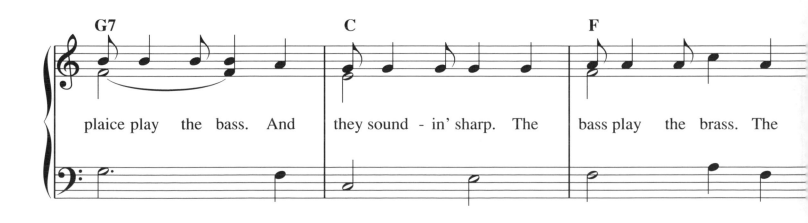

plaice play the bass. And they sound - in' sharp. The bass play the brass. The

chub play the tub. The fluke is the duke of soul. The

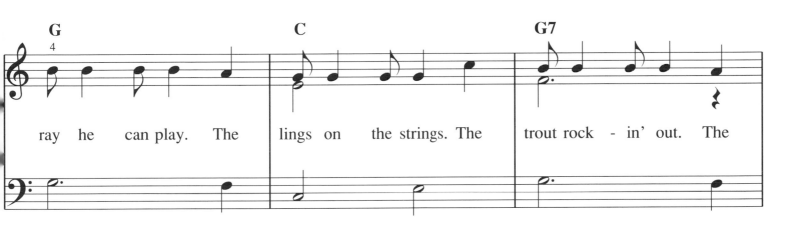

ray he can play. The lings on the strings. The trout rock - in' out. The

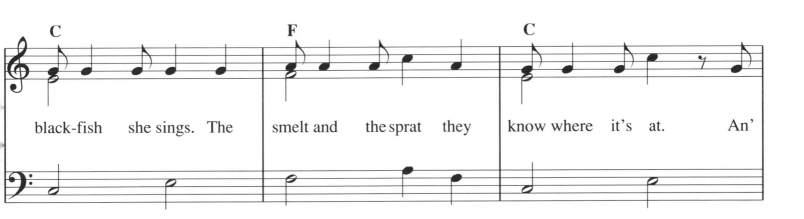

black-fish she sings. The smelt and the sprat they know where it's at. An'

oh, that blow - fish blow.

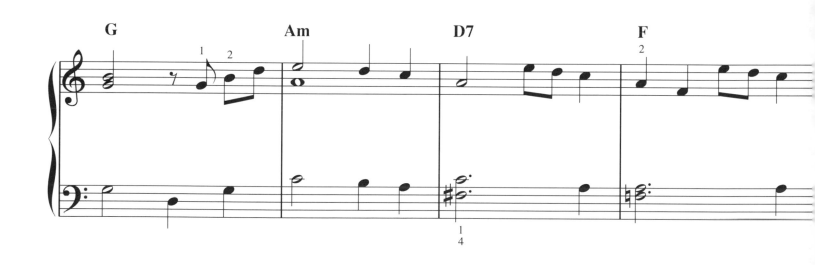

136

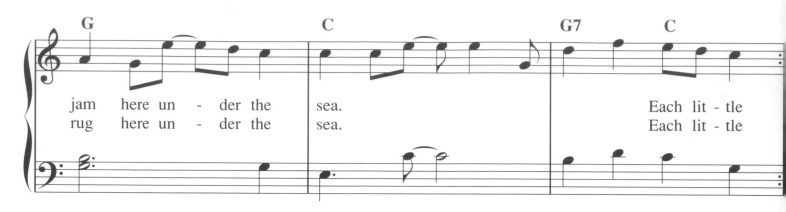

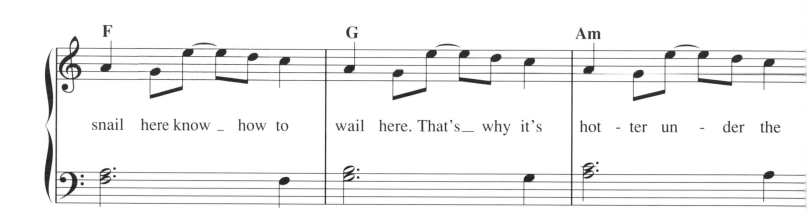

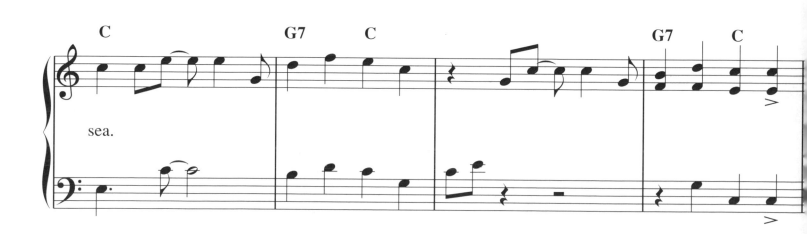

# WHEN I SEE AN ELEPHANT FLY

## (From Walt Disney's "DUMBO")

Words by NED WASHINGTON
Music by OLIVER WALLACE

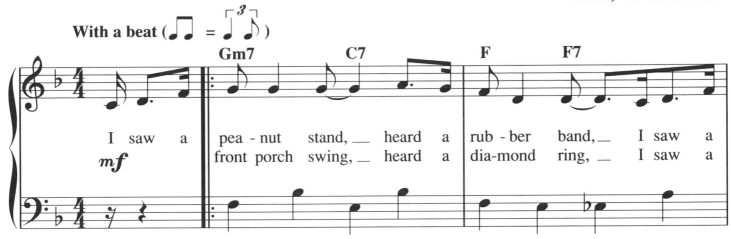

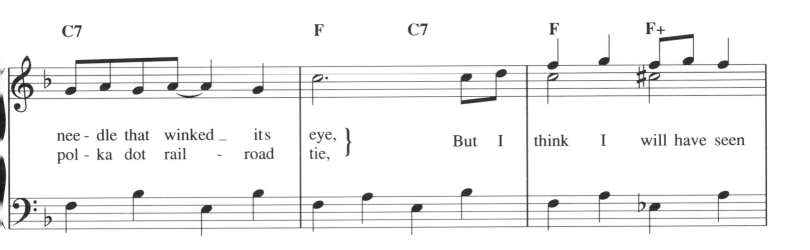

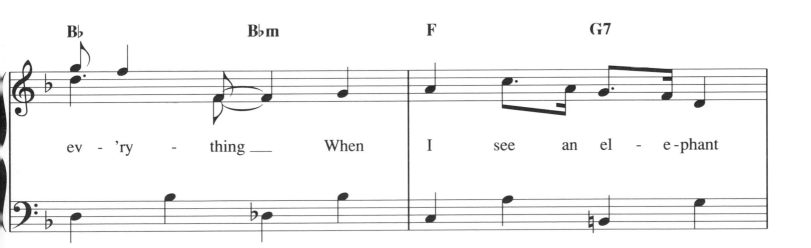

138

139

# WHEN YOU WISH UPON A STAR

## (From Walt Disney's "PINOCCHIO")

Words by NED WASHINGTO
Music by LEIGH HARLI

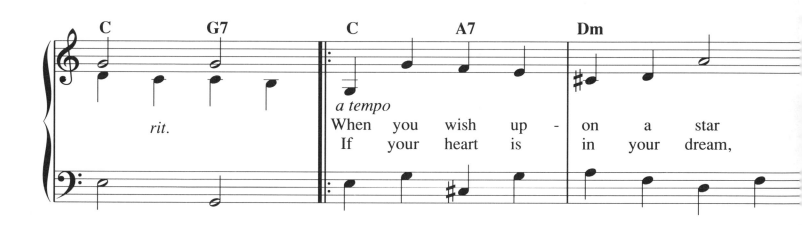

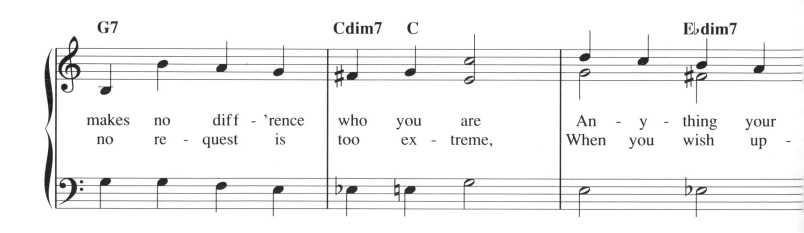

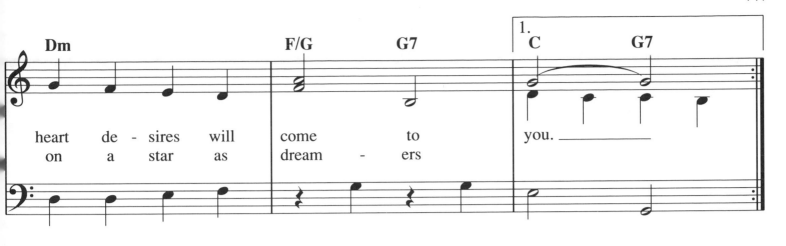

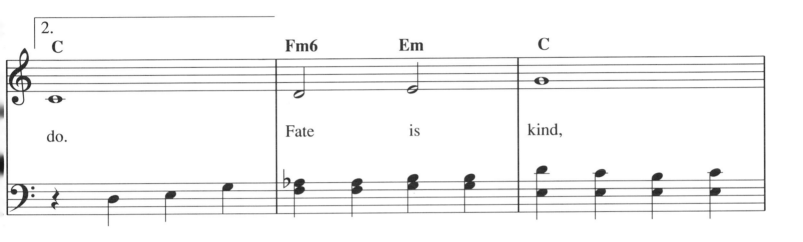

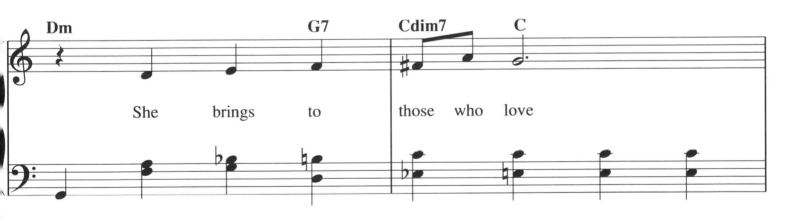

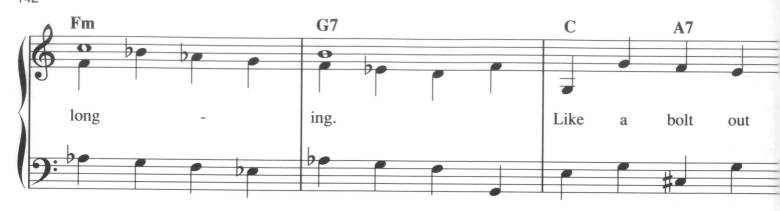

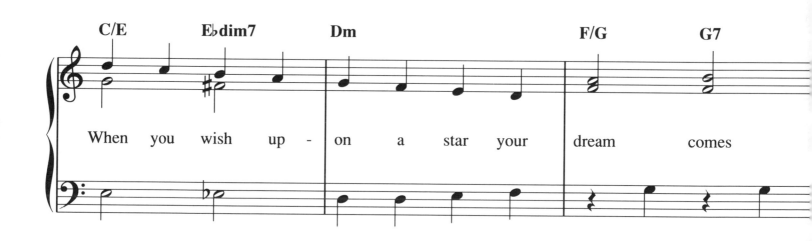

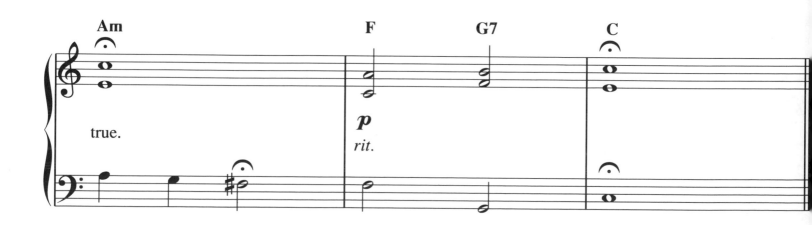

# WHO'S AFRAID OF THE BIG BAD WOLF?
## (From Walt Disney's "THREE LITTLE PIGS")

Words and Music by FRANK CHURCHILL
Additional Lyric by ANN RONELL

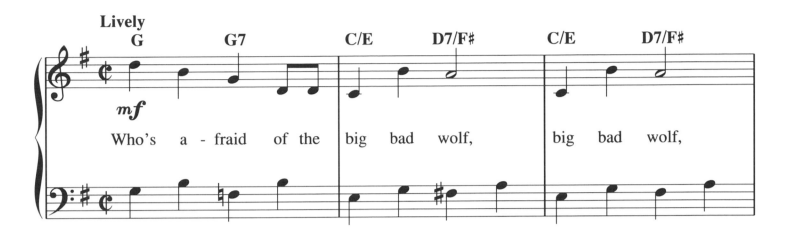

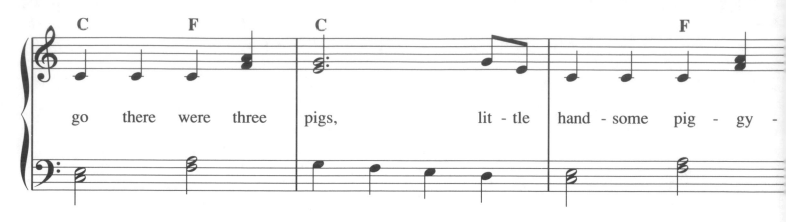

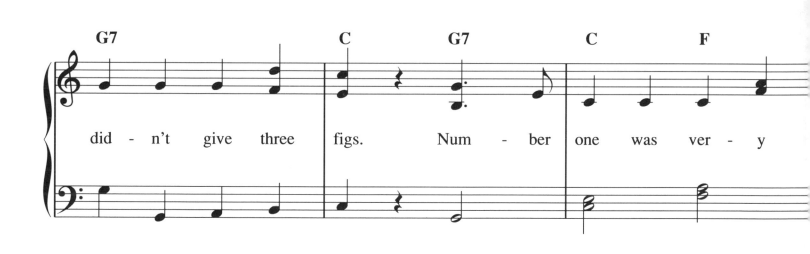

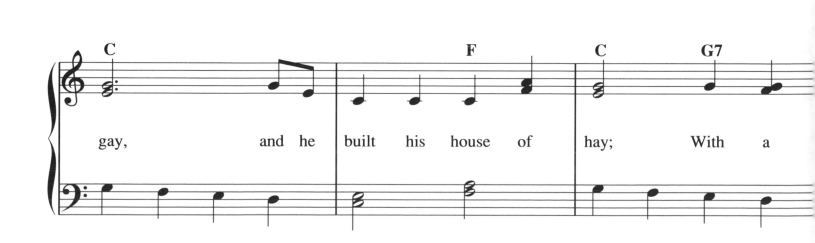

# WHISTLE WHILE YOU WORK

## (From Walt Disney's "SNOW WHITE AND THE SEVEN DWARFS")

Words by LARRY MORE
Music by FRANK CHURCHIL

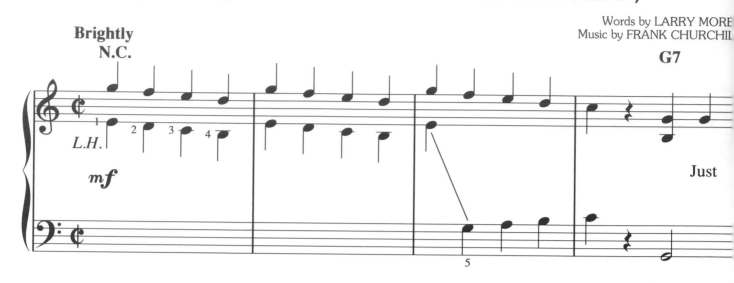

whis - tle while you work,    (whistle)    Put
hum a mer - ry song.    (hum)    Just

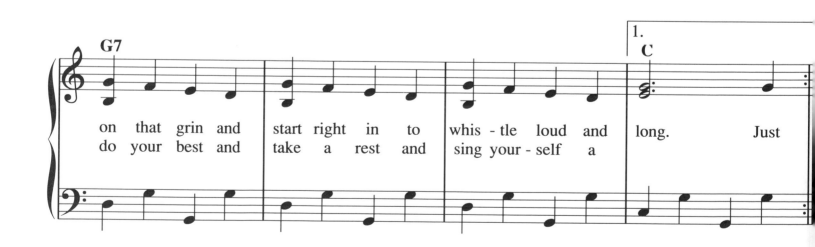

on that grin and    start right in to    whis - tle loud and    long.    Just
do your best and    take a rest and    sing your - self a

song. When there's too much to do don't let it both - er

you; For - get your trou - bles, try to be just like a cheer - ful

chick - a - dee. And whis - tle while you work. *(whistle)* _____ Come

on get smart, tune up and start to whis - tle while you work.

# WINNIE THE POOH

## (From Walt Disney's "WINNIE THE POOH AND THE HONEY TREE")

Words and Music by RICHARD M. SHERMAN
and ROBERT B. SHERMAN

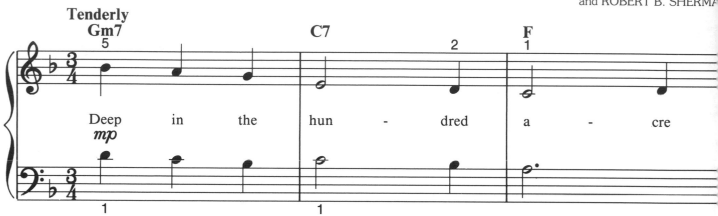

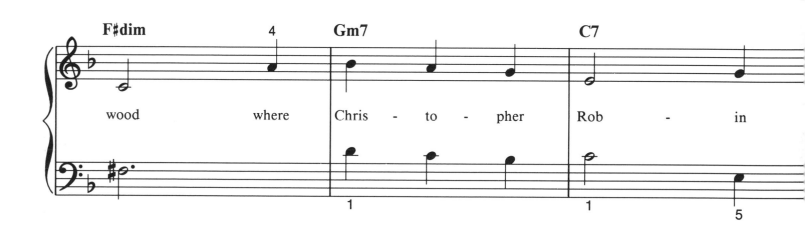

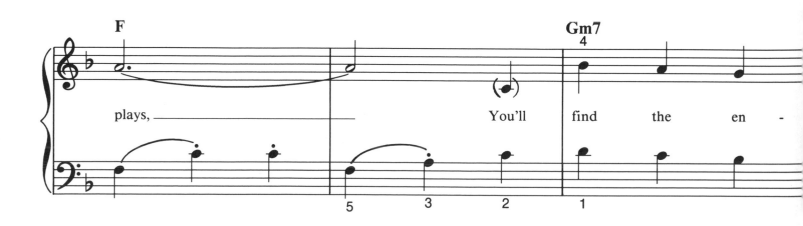

149

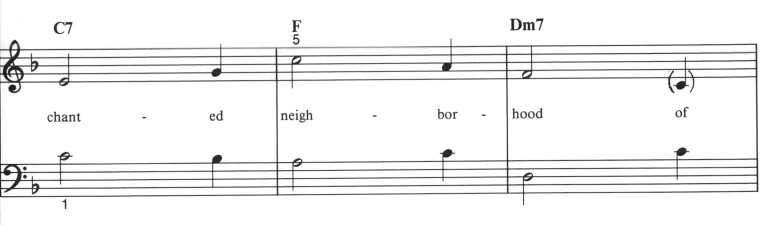

chant - ed neigh - bor - hood of

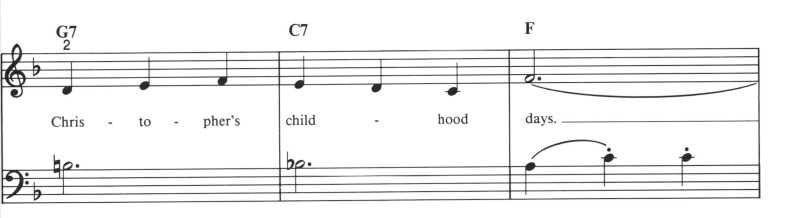

Chris - to - pher's child - hood days.

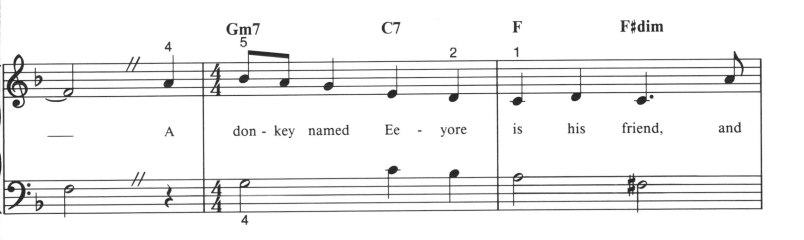

A don - key named Ee - yore is his friend, and

Kan - ga and lit - tle Roo; There's Rab - bit, there's Pig - let

and there's Owl, but most of all Win - nie the Pooh!

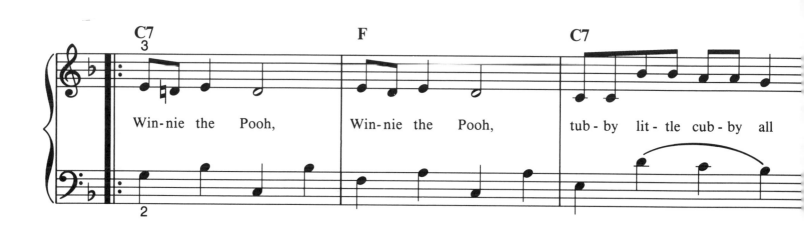

Win - nie the Pooh, Win - nie the Pooh, tub - by lit - tle cub - by all

stuffed with fluff, He's Win - nie the Pooh, Win - nie the Pooh,

wil - ly, nil - ly, sil - ly ole bear. bear.

# WITH A SMILE AND A SONG

## (From Walt Disney's "SNOW WHITE AND THE SEVEN DWARFS")

Words by LARRY MOREY
Music by FRANK CHURCHILL

With a smile and a song,
With a smile and a song,

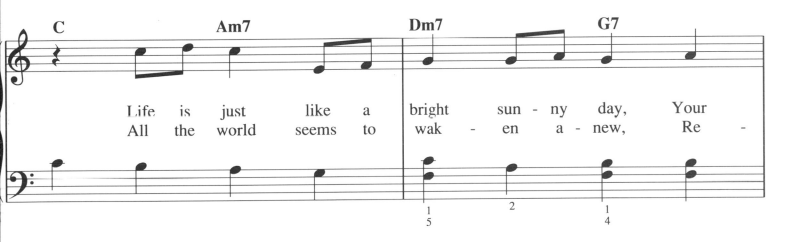

Life is just like a bright sun-ny day, Your
All the world seems to wak - en a - new, Re -

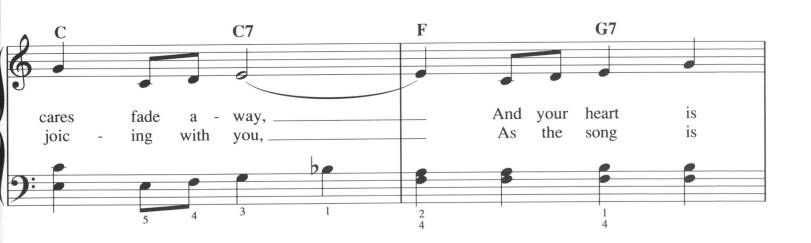

cares fade a - way, And your heart is
joic - ing with you, As the song is

152

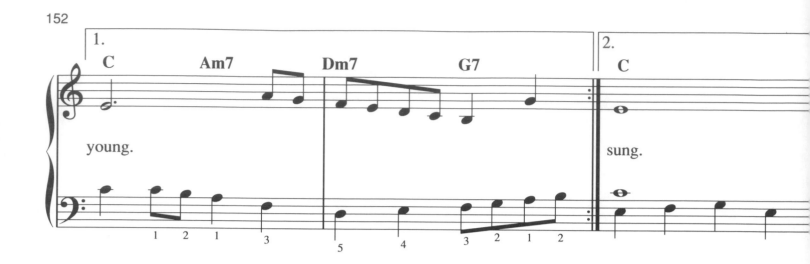

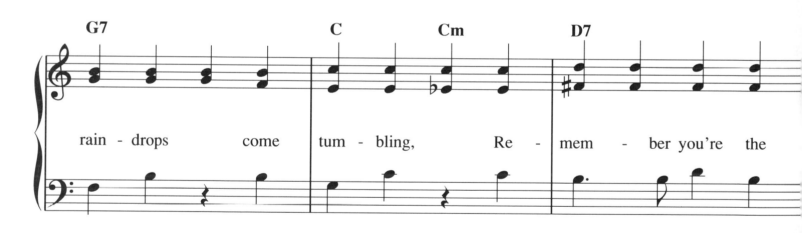

# THE WORK SONG
## (From Walt Disney's "CINDERELLA")

Words and Music by MACK DAVID
AL HOFFMAN and JERRY LIVINGSTON

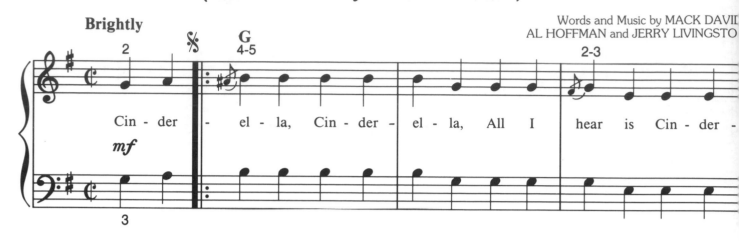

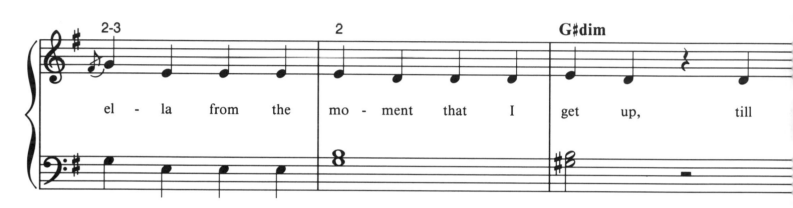

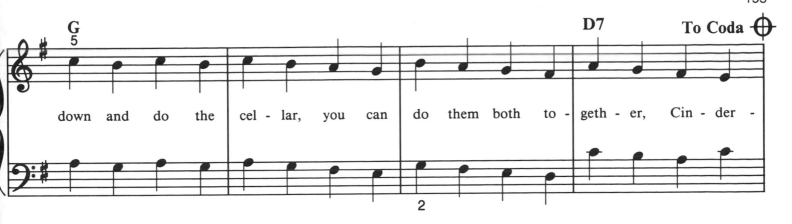

G
D7 To Coda

down and do the cel - lar, you can do them both to - geth - er, Cin - der -

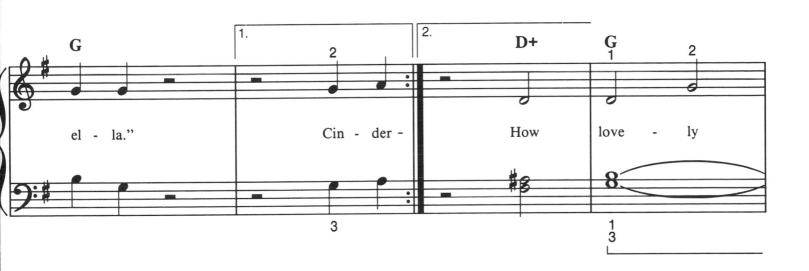

G 1. 2. D+ G

el - la." Cin - der - How love - ly

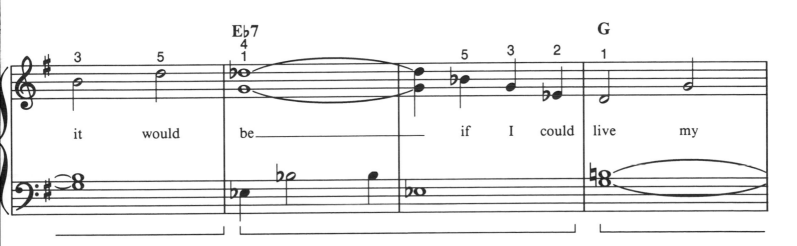

Eb7 G

it would be if I could live my

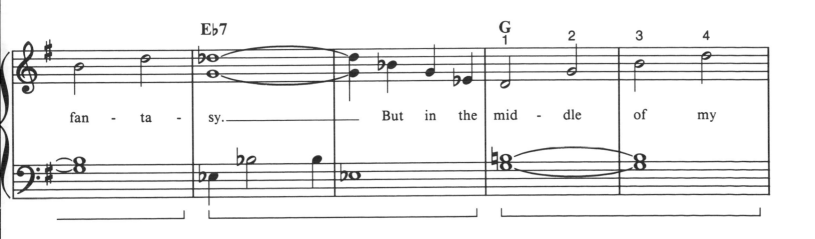

Eb7 G

fan - ta - sy. But in the mid - dle of my

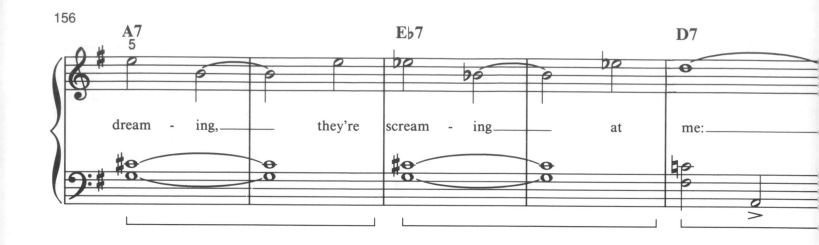

dream - ing,_____ they're scream - ing_____ at me:_____

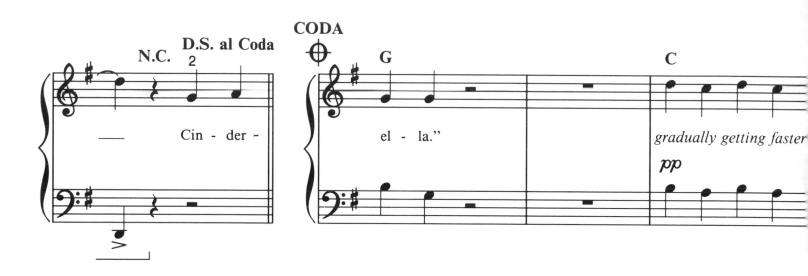

_____ Cin - der -

el - la."

gradually getting faster
*pp*

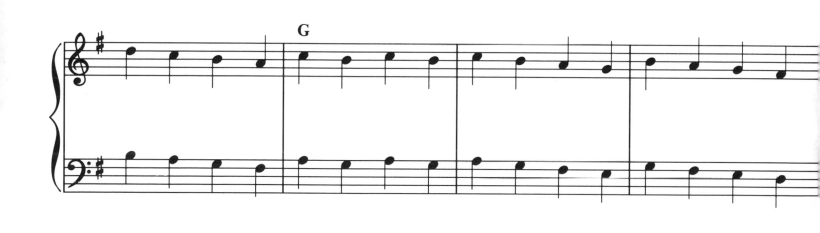

as fast as possible

*8va lower*

# YO HO (A PIRATE'S LIFE FOR ME)

**(From The Disneyland and Walt Disney World Attraction "PIRATES OF THE CARIBBEAN")**

Words by XAVIER ATENCIO
Music by GEORGE BRUNS

**Am**                 **E7**

up     me     'eart - ies,    yo      ho.              { We / Ma - / We

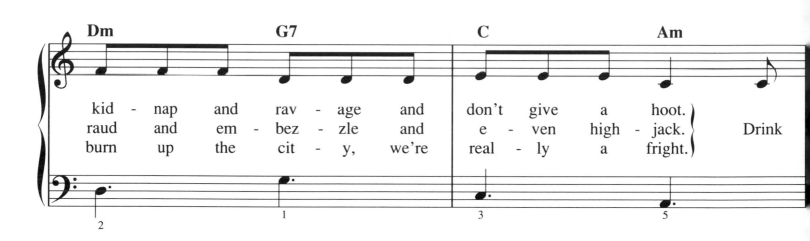

**Dm**           **G7**           **C**           **Am**

kid - nap    and    rav - age    and     don't   give    a     hoot.

raud    and    em - bez - zle    and     e - ven    high - jack.     Drink

burn    up    the    cit - y,    we're    real - ly    a    fright.

2           1           3           5

1.,2.

**D7**                       **G7**

up     me     'eart - ies,    yo      ho.

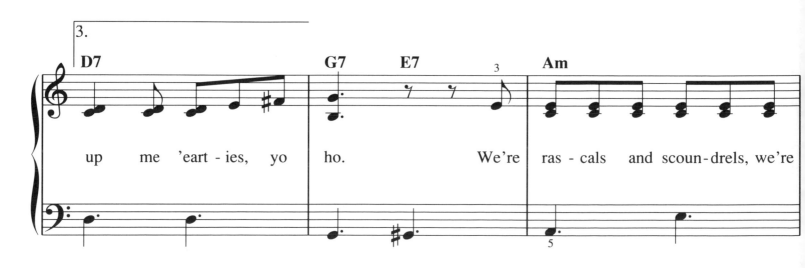

3.

**D7**          **G7**      **E7**     3     **Am**

up     me     'eart - ies,    yo      ho.        We're   ras - cals    and scoun - drels, we're

5

159

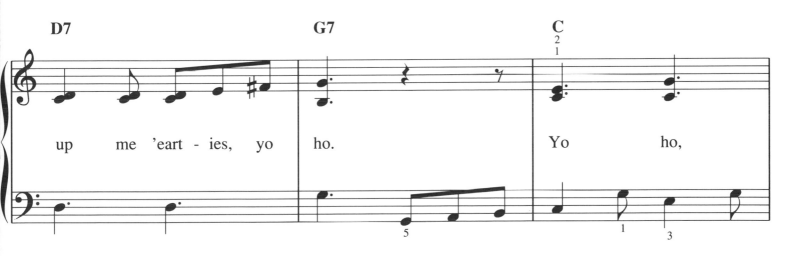

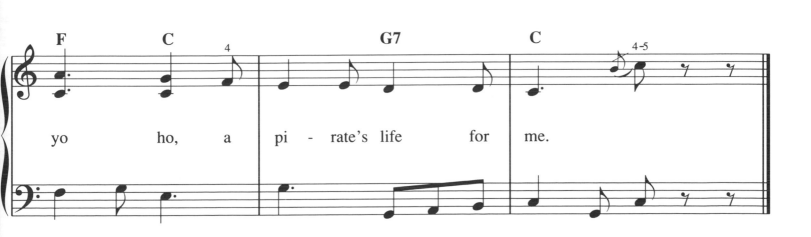

# YOU CAN FLY!
# YOU CAN FLY! YOU CAN FLY!

(From Walt Disney's "PETER PAN")

Words by SAMMY CAHN
Music by SAMMY FAIN

Moderately

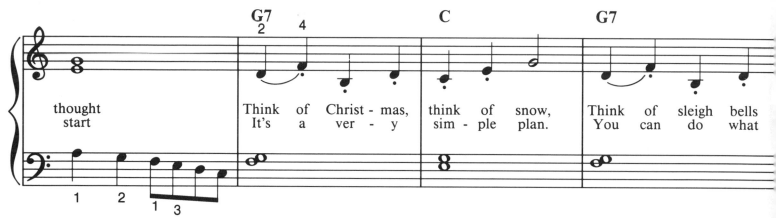

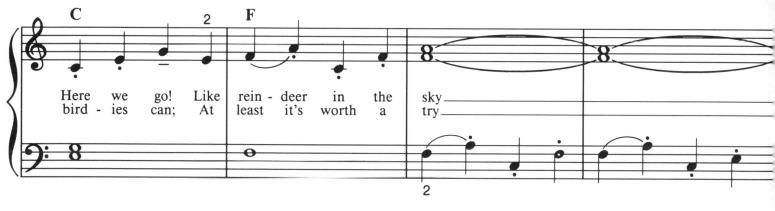

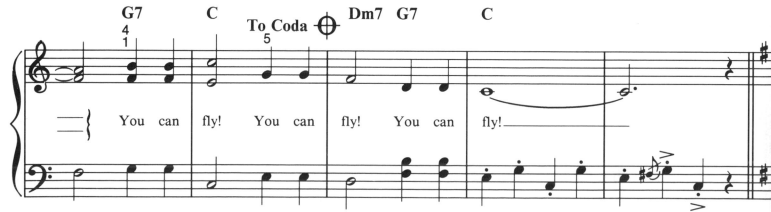

161

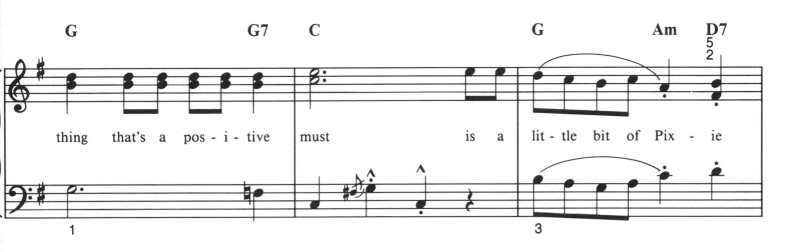

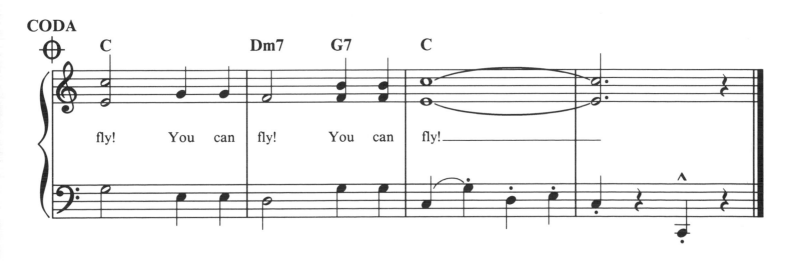

# ZIP-A-DEE-DOO-DAH

## (From Walt Disney's "SONG OF THE SOUTH")

Words by RAY GILBER
Music by ALLIE WRUBE

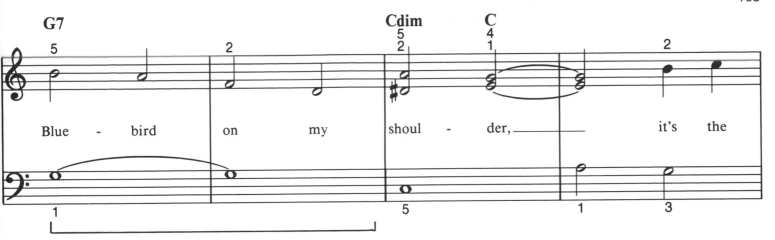

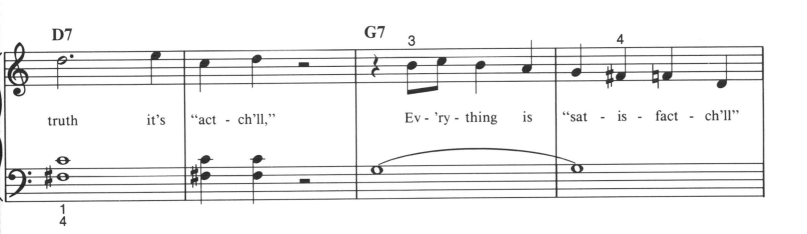

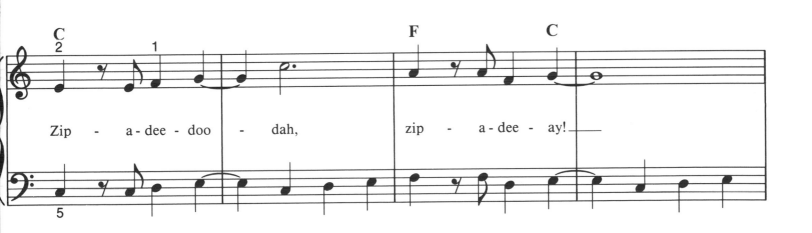

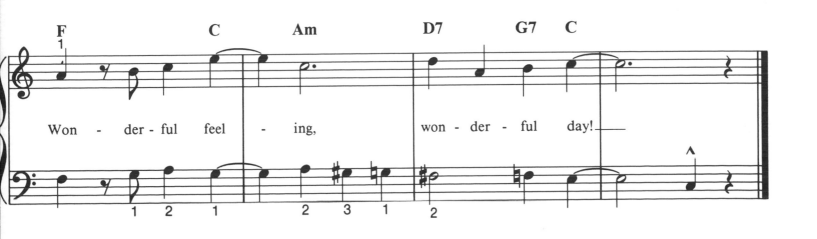

# THEME FROM ZORRO

Words by NORMAN FOST[
Music by GEORGE BRU[

Fast, with excitement

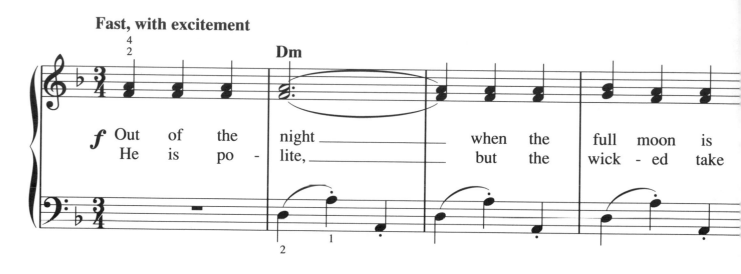

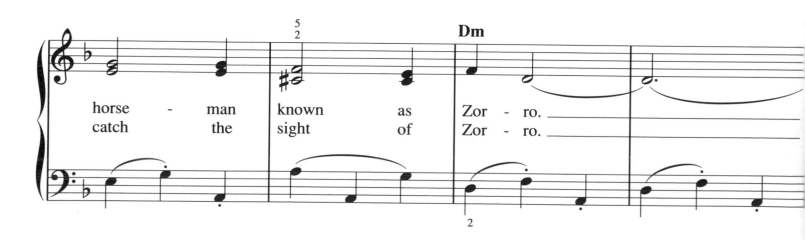

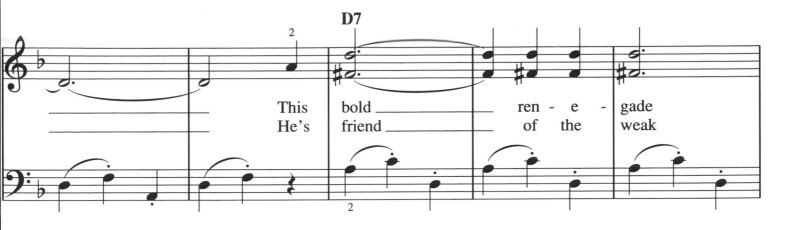

This bold _____ ren - e - gade
He's friend _____ of the weak

carves a Z _____ with his blade, _____ a
and the poor _____ and the meek, _____ this

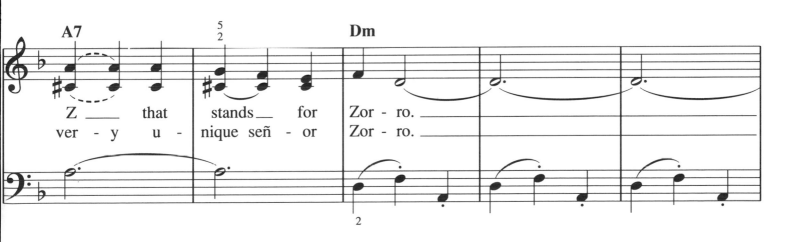

Z ____ that stands ___ for Zor - ro. _____
ver - y u - nique señ - or Zor - ro. _____

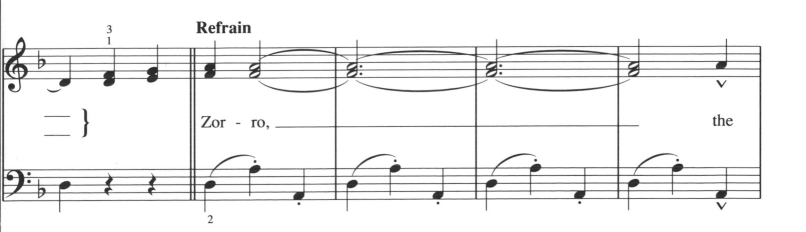

**Refrain**

Zor - ro, _____ the

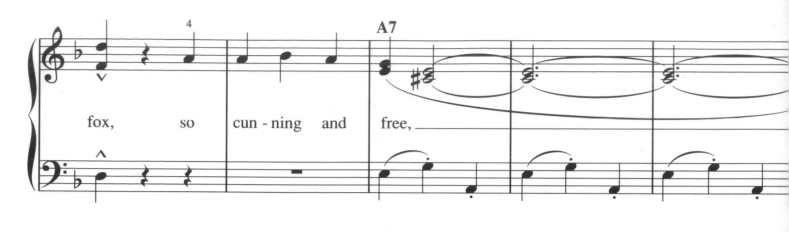

fox, so cun - ning and free, _____

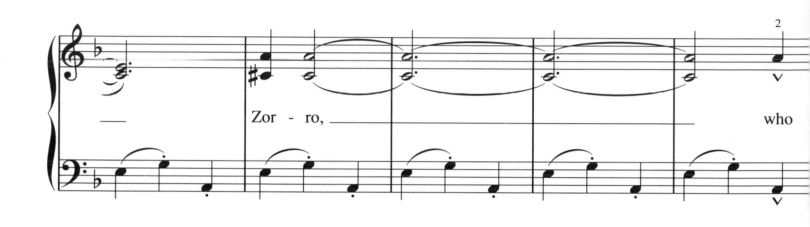

_____ Zor - ro, _____ who

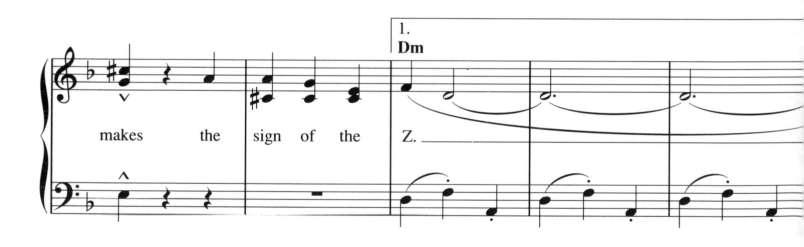

makes the sign of the Z. _____

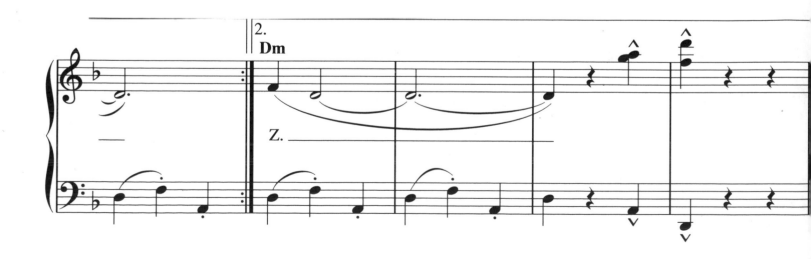

_____ Z. _____